taste.
BAKING

Over 100 mouth-watering recipes

igloo

igloo

Published in 2010
by Igloo Books Ltd
Cottage Farm
Sywell
NN6 0BJ

www.igloo-books.com
Copyright © 2010 Igloo Books Ltd

10 9 8 7 6 5 4 3 2 1
ISBN: 978 1 84852 955 7

Food photography and recipe development: Stockfood, The Food Image Agency
Front and back cover images © Stockfood, The Food Image Agency

Printed and manufactured in China.

contents.

introduction.

Baking is about the most magical thing you can do in the kitchen. Using a few everyday ingredients, you can make wonderful, simple, but delicious things to eat. Add a handful of other basic ingredients, like eggs, milk, butter, sugar and yeast and a myriad of wonderful creations are possible.

Conversely, it is one area of cooking where it is wise to follow recipe instructions to the letter and resist the temptation to improvise. In fact, it is one of the most technical areas of cooking, where small differences in proportions of ingredients, oven temperature and timing can make all the difference. The judgment that comes with experience is critical in baking. So, if you are a novice, take any failures in your stride, learn from them and try again until you get it right. The saving grace of baking is that it's not often that the results, however imperfect, are inedible. The key to success lies in being properly prepared:

1 Carefully read the recipe - obvious, yes, but it will ensure you have enough time and all the ingredients.

2 Ensure that all ingredients, especially raising agents, have not passed best-before dates. (Also, generally eggs and butter should be at room temperature before baking.)

3 Try to use correctly sized pans. (Never fill baking pans or cupcake cases more than two-thirds full. Muffin cases can be filled three-quarters full to create the characteristic 'muffin top'.

4 Get your oven fully preheated, normally even before you start mixing ingredients. Test your oven often regularly for accuracy with a portable oven thermometer.

5 Adjust oven shelves as necessary; especially if using more than one pan. There needs to be enough space above and below pans to allow hot air to circulate around them.

6 Prepare the pans you are going to use even before mixing your ingredients – grease as required, then coat them with flour and tap out any excess.

7 If making pie crusts, puff pastry or croissants, make sure the fats are cold, as this produces the flakiest crusts.

8 Sift all dry ingredients before use. Sifting removes lumps and aerates flour so it is more easily incorporated into the liquid ingredients.

9 Measure ingredients exactly.

10 Check eggs for freshness - crack each into a separate container before adding it to other ingredients. When separating eggs for meringue, make sure you do not get a drop of yolk gets into the whites as this will prevent them from beating up fully. Also ensure your bowl and whisk, etc. are scrupulously clean for the same reason.

11 When creaming butter and sugar, do this until the mixture is light and fluffy, usually at least a good 5 minutes.

12 After adding flour to a mixture, don't overbeat as this will overwork the flour and make results dense. Simply beat or stir until the flour is just incorporated.

13 Ovens vary, so most recipes suggest a range of cooking times. Always bake to the shorter cooking time before opening the oven door, and then check every few minutes until fully cooked.

14 Cakes, cupcakes and muffins are only ready when a skewer or wooden toothpick is inserted into their centre and comes out clean.

15 Let cakes and other items baked in pans or moulds cool in the pan or mould for 10 minutes; then turn them out on a wire rack to cool.

If your cakes are not as good as you hoped There are ways to assess what may have gone wrong so you can get it right next time:

1 If the insides are too dry and crumbly, then your mix may need a little more liquid or a little less raising agent.

2 If hard on the outside but not properly cooked in the middle, then your oven was probably too hot or you positioned the cake too high, or there was too much liquid in your mix.

3 If the insides are heavy and doughy there may have been too much liquid or too little raising agent. Also you may not have creamed fat and flour together well enough.

4 If it sank in the middle, you may not have creamed enough or the oven was too hot.

5 If it developed a dome-shaped top, then you may have used too much raising agent or the oven was too hot.

6 If the surface was very cracked, you may have used too much raising agent or there was too little liquid in the mix, the tin may have been too small or the oven too hot.

The wide range of exciting recipes that follow, arranged in chapters on delicious Cupcakes & Muffins, wonderful Cakes and Bakes, mouth-watering Savoury snacks and Bread & Buns, and tasty treats for Entertaining. Our recipes are well tested and selected to ensure that they will suit both novice cooks and experienced bakers, so you can produce bakes both comforting and spectacular for all sort of occasions.

cupcakes & muffins.

Cupcakes with frosting and flowers

Prep and cook time: 45 minutes
Cannot be frozen
Makes: 24 cupcakes

Ingredients:
For the dough:
1 egg
1 lemon, juiced and zest grated
80 ml | 1/3 cup vegetable oil
120 g | 5/8 cup sugar
1 dash vanilla extract
1 pinch salt
250 ml | 1 cup buttermilk
250 g | 2 cups plain|all purpose flour
2 tsp baking powder
1/2 tsp baking soda

To decorate:
125 g | 1 cup icing|confectioners' sugar
24 small sugar flowers, ready-made

Method:
Heat the oven to 180°C (160°C fan) 375°F, gas 5.

Place 24 paper baking cups in the muffin tray.
Beat the egg with the lemon zest, oil, sugar, vanilla extract, salt and buttermilk. Mix the flour with the baking powder and baking soda. Pour the egg mixture into the flour and beat until all ingredients are moist. Spoon the dough into the paper cups.

Bake for 13-15 minutes on the middle shelf. Test using a wooden toothpick, if it comes out clean, the cakes are done.
Cool the cupcakes on a wire rack.

To decorate, mix the icing/confectioners' sugar with 2-3 tsp lemon juice to make the frosting. It should not be too liquid. Spread the lemon frosting on the cool cupcakes. Decorate with sugar flowers and let the frosting set completely.

Apple muffins

Prep and cook time: 40 minutes
Can be frozen
Makes: 12 muffins

Ingredients:
For the dough:
2 large apples, peeled, cored
and chopped
280 g | 2 ¼ cups plain|all purpose flour
2 tsp baking powder
½ tsp baking soda
1 tsp cinnamon
1 egg
80 g | ⅓ cup sugar
80 ml | ⅓ cup vegetable oil
200 ml | ⅞ cup buttermilk
125 ml | ½ cup apple juice

To decorate:
2 tbsp sugar
1 tsp cinnamon

Method:
Heat the oven to 180°C (160°C fan) 375°F, gas 5.

Butter the cups of the muffin pan. Mix the chopped apple with the flour, baking powder, baking soda and cinnamon in a mixing bowl. Beat the egg in another bowl; beat in the sugar, oil, buttermilk and apple juice. Beat the dry ingredients quickly into the egg mixture until they are all moist. Spoon the dough into the muffin pan.

Bake on the middle shelf for 20-25 minutes until golden brown. Test with a wooden toothpick, if it comes out clean, the muffins are done. Let them cool in the pan for 5 minutes, then place on a wire rack to cool completely.

Dust with sugar and cinnamon to serve.

Chocolate chilli muffins

Prep and cook time: 55 minutes
Can be frozen
Makes: 12 muffins

Ingredients:
For the dough:
200 g | 2 ¼ cups dark chocolate,
60 % cocoa solids, chopped
100 g | ½ cup butter
250 g | 2 cups plain|all purpose flour
2 tsp cornflour|cornstarch
3 tsp baking powder
3 tbsp cocoa powder
1 pinch salt
200 ml | ⅞ cup milk
1 egg
100 ml | 7 tbsp sour cream
100 g | ½ cup sugar
1 red chilli pepper, seeds removed,
very finely chopped

To decorate:
chilli powder, or Cayenne pepper
small red chilli peppers (optional)

Method:
Heat the oven to 180°C (160°C fan) 375°F, gas 5.

Place 12 paper baking cups in the muffin pan.
Place about a quarter of the chocolate in a bowl with the butter and melt over a saucepan of simmering water.

Thoroughly mix the flour, cornflour/cornstarch, baking powder, cocoa powder and salt in a large bowl. In another bowl, beat the milk with the egg, sour cream and sugar. Stir the melted chocolate, the chopped chilli and the remaining chopped chocolate into the egg mixture and add everything to the flour. Beat quickly until the dry ingredients are moist.
Spoon the dough into the paper cups.

Bake on the middle shelf for 20-25 minutes. Test using a wooden toothpick, if it comes out clean, the muffins are done. Cool on a wire rack.

To serve, dust with a little chilli powder. The muffins may be decorated with chilli peppers.

Butterfly buns

Prep and cook time: 1 hour 15 minutes
Cannot be frozen
Makes: 24 buns

Ingredients:
For the dough:
125 g | ½ cup soft butter
120 g | ⅝ cup sugar
2 eggs
200 g |1 cup quark (low-fat soft cheese)
250 g | 2 cups plain|all purpose flour
3 tsp baking powder
300 g | 1 ¼ cups Morello cherries

To decorate:
2 sheets red gelatine
3 tbsp icing|confectioners' sugar
150 g | ¾ cup quark
24 small sponge cookies

Method:
Heat the oven to 180°C (160°C fan) 375°F, gas 5.

Place 24 paper baking cups in the muffin pan. Beat the butter with the sugar until pale and fluffy. Add the eggs and quark. Mix the flour and baking powder. Quickly beat the butter mixture into the flour until all the ingredients are moist. Mix half of the cherries into the dough, reserving the rest for the decoration.

Spoon the dough into the paper cups. Bake on the middle shelf for 15-17 minutes. Test with a wooden toothpick, if it comes out clean, the buns are done. Cool on a wire rack.

To decorate, soften the gelatine in cold water. Puree the reserved cherries with a hand-held mixer. Squeeze out the gelatine and warm gently in a small saucepan with 2 tbsp cherry puree.

Take the saucepan off the heat and stir in the remaining puree. Stir in 1 tbsp icing/confectioners' sugar and the quark. Spread the cherry quark on the buns. Halve the cookies and arrange 2 halves on each bun to resemble butterfly wings. Dust with the remaining icing/confectioners' sugar.

Chocolate marshmallow muffins

Prep and cook time: 1 hour 15 minutes
Cannot be frozen
Makes: 12 muffins

Ingredients:
1 egg
12 small chocolate covered
marshmallows, on a waffle base
45 g | ¼ cup brown sugar
2 tsp vanilla extract
80 ml | ⅓ cup vegetable oil
250 ml | 1 cup buttermilk
250 g | 2 cups plain|all purpose flour
2 ½ tsp baking powder
½ tsp baking soda

Also needed:
100 g | 1 cup mascarpone, or full fat
cream cheese
2 tbsp icing|confectioners' sugar

Method:
Heat the oven to 180°C (160°C fan) 375°F, gas 5.

Butter the muffin pan. Beat the egg in a bowl. Cut off the waffle base from each marshmallow and reserve to decorate. Beat the marshmallows with a fork.

Add half the marshmallow to the egg. Beat in the sugar, vanilla extract, oil and buttermilk. Mix the flour with the baking powder and baking soda. Add the flour to the egg mixture and beat quickly, until the dry ingredients are moist. Spoon the dough into the muffin pan.

Bake on the middle shelf for 20-25 minutes. Test with a wooden toothpick, if it comes out clean, the muffins are done. Let the muffins cool 5 minutes in the pan, then turn out carefully and cool completely on a wire rack.

To serve, beat the mascarpone with the icing/confectioners' sugar. Mix in the remaining marshmallow. Cut the muffins in half horizontally. Spread a little of the marshmallow cream on each muffin base and top with the other half. Spread the rest of the marshmallow cream over the muffins and decorate with the waffle marshmallow bases.

Orange muffins

Prep and cook time: 40 minutes
Cannot be frozen
Makes: 10 muffins

Ingredients:
For the muffins:
75 g | ¾ stick butter, melted
1 egg, lightly beaten
175 ml | ¾ cup plain yoghurt
1 orange, juiced and zest finely grated
½ lemon, juiced
200 g | 1 ⅔ cups plain|all purpose flour
2 tsp baking powder
150 g | ¾ cup sugar
1 tbsp orange marmalade

For the glaze:
1 orange, juiced and zest finely grated
6 tablespoons icing|confectioners' sugar
2 teaspoons orange marmalade

Method:
Heat the oven to 180°C (160°C fan) 375°F, gas 5.
Arrange paper baking cups in a 10 cup muffin tin.

Combine the butter, egg, yoghurt, orange juice and zest and lemon juice in a mixing bowl. Stir in the flour, baking powder and sugar. Gently stir in the marmalade.

Spoon the mixture into the paper cases, almost to the top. Bake for 25 minutes until golden and risen. Leave to stand for 5 minutes, then place on a wire rack to cool.

For the glaze, beat all the ingredients together in a bowl. The mixture should be thick enough to coat the back of a spoon, but still fluid.

Spoon the glaze over the muffins.

Pistachio muffins

Prep and cook time: 45 minutes
Can be frozen
Makes: 12 muffins

For the dough:
125 ml | ½ cup milk
100 g | ¼ cup marzipan paste
60 g | ¼ cup soft butter
3 eggs
200 g | 1 ⅔ cups plain|all purpose flour
1 pinch salt
2 tsp baking powder
½ tsp baking soda
100 g | ¾ cup ground pistachios
70 g | ⅓ cup sugar
1 tsp vanilla extract

Method:

Heat the oven to 180°C (160°C fan) 375°F, gas 5.

Butter the muffin pan.

Warm the milk in a small saucepan and stir in the marzipan paste. Pour into a mixing bowl. Add the soft butter and stir in the eggs.

In another bowl, mix the flour with the salt, baking powder and baking soda. Add the pistachios, sugar and vanilla extract. Beat the dry ingredients quickly into the egg mixture until they are moist. Spoon the dough into the muffin pan.

Bake on the middle shelf for 20-25 minutes until golden brown. Test with a wooden toothpick, if it comes out clean, the muffins are done. Let rest for 5 minutes in the pan, then turn out onto a wire rack to cool completely.

Muffins with strawberry cream

Prep and cook time: 1 hour
Cannot be frozen
Makes: 12 muffins

Ingredients:
For the dough:
250 g | 2 cups plain|all purpose flour
50 g | ⅓ cup ground almonds
2 tsp baking powder
½ tsp baking soda
3 eggs
100 g | ½ cup sugar
12 tsp vanilla extract
80 ml | ⅓ cup vegetable oil
250 ml | 1 cup sour cream

To decorate:
150 g | ½ cup strawberries
1 tbsp icing|confectioners' sugar
150 ml | ⅔ cup cream

Method:

Heat the oven to 180°C (160°C fan) 375°F, gas 5.

Place 12 paper baking cups in the muffin pan. Mix the flour, almonds, baking powder and baking soda in a bowl.
Beat the eggs in a separate bowl and stir in the sugar, vanilla extract, oil and sour cream. Add the flour mix to the egg mixture and beat quickly until all the ingredients are moist.

Spoon the dough into the paper cups. Bake for 20-25 minutes until golden brown. Test using a wooden toothpick, if it comes out clean, the muffins are done. Cool on a wire rack.

To decorate, slice 8 strawberries to garnish and puree the rest with a hand-held mixer. Pass the puree through a sieve and stir in the icing/confectioners' sugar. Whip the cream until stiff and fold into the strawberry puree. Pour the strawberry cream into a piping bag with a star-shaped nozzle and top each muffin with the cream.

Garnish with strawberry slices and serve at once.

Pear and anise muffins

Prep and cook time: 1 hour
Cannot be frozen
Makes: 24 mini muffins

Ingredients:
For the muffin mixture:
1 small can pears
(180 g drained weight)
100 g | ¾ cup plain|all purpose flour
100 g | 1 ⅓ cups rolled oats
50 g | ⅓ cup finely chopped almonds
2 tsp grated lemon rind
1 tsp ground anise
1 ½ tsp baking powder
½ tsp baking soda
1 egg
80 g | ⅜ cup brown sugar
60 ml | ¼ cup vegetable oil
150 ml | ⅔ cup sour cream
butter, for the tin, or 24 small
paper cases

To decorate:
75 ml | ⅓ cup cream, suitable
for whipping
100 g | 1 cup fresh soft cheese
50 g | ⅜ cup icing|confectioners' sugar
2 tsp grated lemon rind
24 whole star anise
whole shelled almonds

Method:
Heat the oven to 180°C (160°C fan) 375°F, gas 5.

Drain the pears (catching the juice) and cut into small pieces. Carefully mix the flour with the rolled oats, chopped pears, almonds, lemon rind, ground anise, baking powder and baking soda.

Lightly beat the egg in a bowl. Add the sugar, oil, sour cream and 80 ml pear juice and mix well. Add the dry ingredients to the egg mixture and mix just long enough to moisten the dry ingredients.

Butter the muffin tin or place a paper baking case in each cup. Spoon the mixture into the tin or the paper cases.

Bake on the middle shelf of the oven for about 15 minutes. Take out of the oven, leave the muffins in the tin for a further 5 minutes, then take out and cool.

To decorate, whip the cream, mix the whipped cream with the soft cheese, icing/confectioners' sugar, 2 tbsp pear juice and the lemon rind and spread roughly on the muffins. Decorate with star anise and almonds.

Christmas cupcakes

Prep and cook time: 1 hour 25 minutes
Cannot be frozen
Makes: 12 cupcakes

Ingredients:
For the dough:
80 g | ²/₃ cups dark chocolate
200 g | 1 ²/₃ cups plain|all purpose flour
2 tbsp cocoa
1 tsp Christmas spice mix
15 g baking powder
50 g | ¼ cup sugar
50 ml | 10 tsp vegetable oil
1 tbsp rum
50 ml | 10 tsp milk,
more if needed
2 eggs

For the decorations:
200 g | ²/₃ cup white chocolate,
chopped
75 ml | ⅓ cup cream
50 g | ¼ cup butter
100 g | ½ cup marzipan paste
1-2 tbsp icing|confectioners' sugar
red food colouring
green sugar strands, or green
decoration sugar

Method:

Heat the oven to 200°C (180°C fan) 400°F, gas 6.

Place 12 paper baking cups in the muffin pan. Mix the chocolate with the flour, cocoa powder, spice mix and the baking powder. Beat the eggs with the sugar and oil. Quickly beat the flour mixture into the eggs, adding the rum and as much milk as required to achieve a dropping consistency.

Spoon the dough into the paper cups in the muffin tin. Bake on the middle shelf for 20-25 minutes. Test with a wooden toothpick, if it comes out clean, the muffins are done. Cool on a wire rack.

For the decorations, place the white chocolate in a bowl. Bring the cream to a boil, let cool slightly and pour over the chocolate. Stir until the chocolate has melted. Add the butter and beat until the mixture is glossy. Chill in the fridge until half set.

Knead the marzipan paste with the icing/confectioners' sugar and the food color, until the marzipan is dark red. Roll out the marzipan paste on a surface dusted with icing/confectioners' sugar to about 5 mm / ¼" thick and cut out 12 small stars. Roll the remaining marzipan to a thin roll, chop into equal pieces and roll these into little balls.

Spoon the semi-set chocolate cream into a piping bag and top the muffins with swirls of chocolate cream. Decorate with the marzipan stars and balls and the green sugar strands.

Berry muffins with cream topping and mint sprigs

Prep and cook time: 1 hour 15 minutes
Cannot be frozen
Makes: 12 muffins

Ingredients:
For the filling:
100 g | ³/₈ cup full fat cream cheese
1 tbsp cream
2 tbsp sugar
50 g | ¹/₃ cup strawberries, chopped

For the dough:
250 g | 2 cups plain|all purpose flour
2 ¹/₂ tsp baking powder
¹/₂ tsp baking soda
1 egg
100 g | ¹/₂ cup sugar
80 ml | ¹/₃ cup vegetable oil
100 ml | 7 tbsp cream
150 ml | ²/₃ cup buttermilk

For the topping:
1 sheet red gelatine
200 g | 1 ¹/₄ cups strawberries
100 ml | 7 tbsp cream
12 mint sprigs
2 tbsp icing|confectioners' sugar

Method:
Heat the oven to 180°C (160°C fan) 375°F, gas 5.
Place 12 paper baking cups in the muffin pan.

For the filling, beat the cream cheese with the cream and sugar.

For the dough, mix the flour with the baking powder and baking soda. Beat the egg in a bowl; beat in the sugar, oil, cream and buttermilk. Add the flour mix and beat quickly until the dry ingredients are moist.

Spoon half the dough into the paper cups. Spoon on the cream cheese mixture and the strawberries, then top with the remaining dough.

Bake on the middle shelf for 20-25 minutes until golden brown. Test with a wooden toothpick, if it comes out clean, the muffins are done. Take the muffins out of the pan and let cool completely on a wire rack.

For the topping, soften the red gelatine in cold water. Puree the strawberries with a hand-held mixer and pass through a sieve. Squeeze out the gelatine and warm in a small saucepan with 2 tbsp strawberry puree. Take the saucepan off the heat and gradually stir in the remaining strawberry puree.

To serve, whip the cream until stiff. Top each of the muffins with strawberry sauce and cream. Decorate with mint sprigs and dust with icing/confectioners' sugar.

Cupcakes with cream and violets

Prep and cook time: 1 hour 10 minutes
Cannot be frozen
Makes: 24 cupcakes

Ingredients:
For the dough:
1 egg
25 g | 1 tbsp candied ginger, chopped
1 lime, juiced and zest grated
125 g | ⁵⁄₈ cup sugar
80 ml | ¹⁄₃ cup vegetable oil
250 ml | 1 cup buttermilk
250 g | 2 cups plain|all purpose flour
2 tsp baking powder
½ tsp baking soda

For the topping:
150 ml | ²⁄₃ cup cream
2 tbsp icing|confectioners' sugar
24 violet flowers

Method:
Heat the oven to 180°C (160°C fan) 375°F, gas 5.

Place 24 paper baking cups in the muffin pan. Beat the egg with the candied ginger and lime zest. Beat in the sugar, oil, buttermilk and 2 tbsp lime juice. Mix the flour with the baking powder and baking soda in a bowl. Beat the egg mixture into the flour until all the ingredients are moist.

Spoon the dough into the paper cups. Bake on the middle shelf for 25 minutes until golden brown. Test with a wooden toothpick, if it comes out clean, the cakes are done. Cool on a wire rack.

To serve, whip the cream until stiff. Fold in the icing/confectioners' sugar. Spoon the cream into a piping bag and top the cupcakes with cream. Decorate with violet flowers.

Strawberry muffins

Prep and cook time: 50 minutes
Cannot be frozen
Makes: 12 muffins

Ingredients:
For the dough:
150 g 1 cup strawberries, chopped
250 g | 2 cups plain|all purpose flour
2 ¹/₂ tsp baking powder
¹/₂ tsp baking soda
100 g | 1 cup sugar
80 ml | ¹/₃ cup vegetable oil
120 ml | ¹/₂ cup cream
120 ml | ¹/₂ cup buttermilk
1 egg

To decorate:
2 tbsp icing|confectioners' sugar

Method:

Heat the oven to 180°C (160°C fan) 375°F, gas 5.

Place the paper cups in the muffin pan. Mix the chopped strawberries with the flour, baking powder and baking soda.

Beat the sugar, oil, cream and buttermilk with the egg. Beat the flour mixture quickly into the egg mixture until the dry ingredients are moist. Spoon the dough into the paper cups.

Bake on the middle shelf for 25-30 minutes. Test with a wooden toothpick, if it comes out clean, the muffins are done. Cool on a wire rack.

To serve, dust with icing/confectioners' sugar.

Bee-sting muffins

Prep and cook time: 1 hour 15 minutes
Cannot be frozen
Makes: 24 muffins

Ingredients:

For the dough:
275 g | 2 ¼ cups plain|all purpose flour
2 tsp baking powder
1 tsp baking soda
3 tbsp cocoa powder
1 egg
130 g | ⅔ cup sugar
80 ml | ⅓ cup vegetable oil
300 ml | 1 ⅓ cups buttermilk

For the filling:
100 g | ½ cup full fat cream cheese
2 tbsp icing|confectioners' sugar
½ tsp lemon zest
1 tsp vanilla extract

For the topping:
1 tbsp honey
100 g | ½ cup sugar
100 g | 1 ¼ cups flaked|slivered almonds

Method:

Heat the oven to 180°C (160°C fan) 375°F, gas 5.

Butter the muffin pan. Mix the flour with the baking powder, baking soda and cocoa powder. Beat the egg in a mixing bowl; beat in the sugar, oil and buttermilk. Add the dry ingredients and beat quickly until the dry ingredients are moist. Spoon 1 tbsp dough into each muffin cup.

Bake on the middle shelf for 12-15 minutes. Test with a wooden toothpick, if it comes out clean, the muffins are done. Let cool for 5 minutes in the pan, then turn out and cool completely on a wire rack.

For the filling, beat the cream cheese with the icing/confectioners' sugar, lemon zest and vanilla extract.

For the topping, melt the honey and sugar in a small saucepan over low to medium heat. Stir in the flaked/slivered almonds and keep warm over a very low heat.

When cool, cut the muffins in half horizontally. Spread some of the cream cheese mix onto the bottom halves and top with the other halves. Spoon the honeyed almonds on top and let cool completely.

Lemon muffins

Prep and cook time: 40 minutes
Can be frozen
Makes: 12 muffins

Ingredients:
2 organic lemons
250 g | 2 cups plain|all purpose flour
3 tsp baking powder
1 tsp vanilla extract
1 pinch salt
125 g | 5/8 cup soft butter
200 g | 1 cup sugar
2 eggs
250 ml | 1 cup yoghurt

Method:

Heat the oven to 180°C (160°C fan) 375°F, gas 5.

Place the paper baking cups in the muffin pan. Grate the zest and squeeze the juice of one lemon. Cut zest strips from the second lemon and squeeze the juice. Reserve the strips for decoration.

Mix the flour, baking powder, vanilla extract, grated lemon zest and salt in a mixing bowl. Beat the butter and sugar in another bowl until creamy. Beat in the lemon juice, eggs and yoghurt. Pour the egg mixture into the dry ingredients and beat quickly until the dry ingredients are moist. Spoon the dough into the paper cups.

Bake on the middle shelf for 20-25 minutes until golden brown. Take out of the pan and place on a wire rack to cool.

To serve, decorate with strips of lemon zest.

White chocolate muffins

Prep and cook time: 1 hour
Can be frozen
Makes: 12 muffins

Ingredients:
200 g | 1 cup sugar
100 ml | 7 tbsp cream
20 g | 1 ½ tbsp butter
1 vanilla pod, scraped out seeds
200 g | 1¾ cups flour
2 tsp baking powder
2 tbsp cornflour|cornstarch
1 small ripe banana
1 pinch salt
3 eggs

In addition:
butter, for the muffin pan
12 paper baking cups

To decorate:
200 g | ½ pound white chocolate
1 tbsp butter
1 tsp vanilla essence
1-2 tbsp cream
white chocolate shavings

Method:

Heat the oven to 180°C (160°C fan) 375°F, gas 5. Line the cups of the muffin pan with paper baking cups.

Put 125 g / ⅔ cup sugar, the cream and butter into a pan and bring to a boil. Add the seeds from the vanilla pod and simmer over a low heat for 5 minutes. Then cool.

Mix the flour, baking powder and cornflour/cornstarch. Peel and puree the banana and whisk into the vanilla cream with the rest of the sugar and the salt. Beat in the eggs. Quickly stir in the flour mixture.

Put the mixture into the lined muffin pan. Bake on the middle shelf of the oven for 30 minutes. Take out of the oven and let cool in the muffin pan for 5 minutes, then take out and cool on a wire rack.

Melt the white chocolate over a bain marie. Mix smoothly with the cream and vanilla and trickle tablespoonfuls over the muffins. Decorate with chocolate shavings and let to cool completely.

Love-heart muffins

Prep and cook time: 40 minutes
Cannot be frozen
Makes: 24 muffins

Ingredients:
For the dough:
200 g | 1 ²/₃ cups plain|all purpose flour
2 tsp baking powder
¹/₂ tsp baking soda
1 egg
75 g ³/₈ cup sugar
2 tsp vanilla extract
70 ml | 14 tsp vegetable oil
250 ml | 1 cup yoghurt

For the topping:
150 ml | ²/₃ cup cream
2 tbsp sugar strands
24 small marshmallow hearts

Method:
Heat the oven to 180°C (160°C fan) 375°F, gas 5.

Place 24 paper baking cups in the muffin pan. Mix the flour with the baking powder and baking soda in a mixing bowl. In another bowl, beat the egg thoroughly with the sugar, vanilla extract, oil and yoghurt. Add the egg mixture to the flour and beat quickly until the dry ingredients are moist.

Spoon the dough into the paper cups and bake on the middle shelf for 13-15 minutes. Test with a wooden toothpick, if it comes out clean, the muffins are done. Cool on a wire rack.

To serve, whip the cream until stiff and fill into a piping bag with a large star-shaped nozzle. Top the muffins with cream and sprinkle with sugar strands. Decorate each with one marshmallow heart.

Raspberry muffins

Prep and cook time: 40 minutes
Cannot be frozen
Makes: 12 muffins

Ingredients:
For the dough:
120 g | ⁵/₈ cup soft butter
120 g | ⁵/₈ cup sugar
1 egg
250 g | 2 cups plain|all purpose flour
2 ¹/₂ tsp baking powder
¹/₂ tsp baking soda
300 ml | 1¹/₃ cups sour cream
200 g | 1¹/₂ cups raspberries,
defrosted if frozen

To decorate:
1 - 2 tbsp icing|confectioners' sugar

Method:
Heat the oven to 180°C (160°C fan) 375°F, gas 5.

Butter the cups in the muffin pan. Beat the butter with the sugar until creamy, then beat in the egg. Mix the flour, a pinch of salt, baking powder and baking soda. Stir the flour mixture and the sour cream into the butter/egg mixture and beat until the dry ingredients are moist. Fold in the raspberries.

Spoon the dough into the muffin pan and bake on the middle shelf for 20-25 minutes until golden brown. Test with a wooden toothpick, if it comes out clean, the muffins are done. Let cool 5 minutes in the pan, then let cool completely on a wire rack.

Dust with icing/confectioners' sugar to serve.

Cupcakes with pink frosting

Prep and cook time: 1 hour
Cannot be frozen
Makes: 24 cupcakes

Ingredients:
For the dough:
1 egg
80 ml | ⅓ cup vegetable oil
130 g | ⅝ cup sugar
1 pinch salt
50 g | ¼ cup cream cheese
220 ml | ⅞ cup buttermilk
250 g | 2 cups plain|all purpose flour
2 tsp baking powder
½ tsp baking soda
75 g | ½ cup raspberries,
defrosted if frozen

For the topping:
75 g | ½ cup raspberries,
defrosted if frozen
100 g | ½ cup cream cheese
1 tbsp icing|confectioners' sugar
2 tbsp sugar strands

Method:
Heat the oven to 180°C (160°C fan) 375°F, gas 5.

Place 24 paper baking cups in the muffin pan. Beat the egg with the oil, sugar, salt, cream cheese and buttermilk. Mix the flour with the baking powder and baking soda. Beat the egg mixture into the flour quickly, until all the ingredients are moist.

Spoon half the dough into the paper cups until half full. Place 1-2 raspberries on each. Spoon the remaining dough on top. Bake on the middle shelf for 13-15 minutes. Test with a wooden toothpick, if it comes out clean, the cupcakes are done. Cool on a wire rack.

For the topping, puree the raspberries with a hand-held mixer. Press the puree through a sieve. Mix the raspberry puree with the cream cheese and sugar until smooth and spoon into a piping bag with a star-shaped nozzle.

Squeeze the raspberry cream onto the cupcakes and sprinkle with sugar strands.

Red velvet cupcakes with redcurrants

Prep and cook time: 1 hour 15 minutes
Cannot be frozen
Makes: 12 cupcakes

Ingredients:
For the dough:
300 g | 2 ⅓ cups plain|all purpose flour
15 g | 3 tsp baking powder
1 tsp baking soda
1 egg
150 ml | ⅔ cup redcurrant syrup,
ready-made

For the topping:
½ vanilla pod, slit open, seeds
scraped out
125 ml | ½ cup milk
1 egg yolk
30 g | ⅛ cup sugar
1 - 2 tsp cornflour|cornstarch
150 ml | ⅔ cup cream

To decorate:
24 mini heart-shaped
cookies, ready-made
12 small bunches redcurrants

Method:
Heat the oven to 180°C (160°C fan) 375°F, gas 5.

Place the paper cups in the muffin pan. Mix the flour with baking powder and baking soda. Beat the egg and stir in the red currant syrup. Add the flour to the egg mixture and beat in quickly.

Spoon the dough into the paper cups and bake on the middle shelf for 20-25 minutes, test with a wooden toothpick, if it comes out clean, the cupcakes are done. Cool on a wire rack.

For the topping, boil the vanilla seeds and the pod with the milk in a small saucepan. Take off the heat and remove the pod. Beat the egg yolk with the sugar until creamy; beat in the cornflour/cornstarch.

Slowly stir the warm milk into the egg yolk, then pour the liquid back into the saucepan. Stir the vanilla cream over a low heat until it thickens; do not boil. Cover with cling film to prevent a skin forming. Let cool.

Whip the cream until stiff and fold into the vanilla cream.

To serve, top the cupcakes with vanilla cream and decorate with two heart-shaped cookies and a small bunch of redcurrants.

desserts.

Lemon soufflé

Prep and cook time: 45 minutes
Cannot be frozen
Serves: 4

Ingredients:
2 tbsp butter
100 g | ½ cup sugar
2 egg yolks
100 g | ½ cup quark
(low-fat cream cheese)
1 pinch lemon zest
3 egg whites
1 tsp plain | all purpose flour

Method:

Heat the oven to 200°C (180°C) 400°F, gas 6. Carefully butter 4 small soufflé dishes and sprinkle with 10 g sugar.

Beat the egg yolks with 75 g / ⅜ cup sugar until white and creamy. Pass the quark through a sieve and mix into the egg yolk mixture with the lemon juice and zest.

Beat the egg whites until stiff, gradually adding 20 g / ⅛ cup sugar. Spoon one third of the egg white onto the egg yolk mixture, sieve the flour over and fold in carefully. Fold the rest of the egg white in carefully.

Spoon the mixture into the soufflé dishes, filling them to ⅔. Wipe away the butter and sugar from the upper rim.

Bake the soufflés for 10-15 minutes and serve at once.

Pumpkin pie

Prep and cook time: 1 hour 40 minutes
Can be frozen
Serves: 8-10

Ingredients:
For the pastry:
250 g | 2 cups plain|all purpose flour
1 tbsp sugar
½ tsp salt
125 g | ½ cup cold butter
1 egg
1 ½ tbsp fruit vinegar

For the filling:
500 g | 1 ¼ pound pumpkin, prepared weight
50 g | ¼ cup butter
1 tsp cinnamon
1 good pinch grated nutmeg
1 good pinch ground cloves
6 tbsp maple syrup
100 ml | 7 tbsp milk
50 g | ¼ cup sugar
4 tbsp whipping cream
40 g | ⅓ cup cornflour|cornstarch
3 eggs, separated
2 tbsp cranberries
1 tsp sugar

Method:

For the pastry, put the flour in a heap on a work surface, mix with the sugar and salt and make a well in the middle of the flour. Cut the butter into small pieces and scatter around the well. Break the egg into the middle, add the vinegar and approximately 50 ml / ¼ cup lukewarm water and chop all the ingredients with a knife until they resemble breadcrumbs.

Quickly combine to a dough using your hands, form into a ball, wrap in cling film and chill for 30 minutes.

Roughly dice the pumpkin. Melt the butter, add the pumpkin, spices (cinnamon, nutmeg, cloves) and maple syrup and sweat briefly, stirring. Add the milk, cover and cook for 10 minutes, or until the pumpkin is soft. Mix the pumpkin to a puree and leave to cool.

Preheat the oven to 200°C (180°C fan) 400°F, gas 6.

Knead the dough briefly and roll out between 2 sheets of baking parchment to a circle a little bigger than the pie dish. Line the pie dish with the pastry and cut off the excess pastry at the edge. Prick the pastry several times with a fork.

Mix the pumpkin puree with the sugar, cream, cornflour/cornstarch and egg yolks. Beat the egg whites until stiff and fold into the pumpkin puree. Spread the mixture smoothly in the pastry case and bake for 35-40 minutes.

Take out of the oven and leave to cool. Before serving, mix the cranberries with the sugar. Place in the middle of the pumpkin pie and serve.

Chocolate cake

Prep and cook time: 1 hour 15 minutes
Can be frozen
Serves: 8-10

Ingredients:
For the dough:
250 g | 1 ⅛ cups butter, chopped
200 g | 2 cups dark chocolate, at least
55 % cocoa solids, chopped
6 eggs, separated
1 lemon, zest and juice
1 vanilla pod, slit open,
seeds scraped out
100 g | ½ cup sugar
75 g | ¼ cup pine nuts
2 tbsp cornflour|cornstarch

To decorate:
2 tbsp icing|confectioners' sugar

Method:
Heat the oven to 180°C (160°C fan) 375°F, gas 5.

Melt the butter and chocolate in a bowl over a saucepan of simmering water. Beat the egg whites stiffly, adding 1 tbsp lemon juice. Mix the vanilla seeds with the egg yolks, sugar and lemon zest and beat until pale and creamy.

Gradually stir in the melted butter and chocolate. Stir in the pine nuts. Spoon the egg whites over the mixture, sift the cornflour/cornstarch over and fold both in carefully.

Butter the pan and dust with flour. Place the chocolate dough in the pan and smooth the top. Bake on the bottom shelf for 40-45 minutes. Test with a wooden toothpick, if it comes out clean, the cake is done. Let cool in the pan for 10 minutes, then carefully remove from the pan and let cool completely.

To serve, dust the cake with icing/confectioners' sugar.

Individual Black Forest gateaux

Prep and cook time: 55 minutes
Cannot be frozen
Makes: 12 gateaux

Ingredients:
2 eggs, separated
50 g | ¼ cup soft butter
80 g | ⅓ cup sugar
125 g | ½ cup milk chocolate, chopped
125 ml | ½ cup milk
120 g | 1 cup plain|all purpose flour
1 tsp cream of tartar

For the filling and topping:
4 tbsp cherry liqueur
600 g | 2 ½ cups Morello cherries
250 ml | 1 cup cream, 30% fat content
1 tbsp icing|confectioners' sugar

to garnish:
2 tbsp chocolate shavings
cinnamon powder
cocoa powder

Method:

Beat the egg yolks, butter, 40 g / ¼ cup sugar and a pinch of salt until creamy. Melt the chocolate in a metal bowl over a saucepan of simmering water and stir into the cream. Gradually mix in the milk.

Beat the egg whites with the remaining sugar until stiff. Mix the flour and cream of tartar. Fold the egg whites and the flour alternately into the chocolate mixture.

Heat the oven to 200°C (180°C fan) 400°F, gas 6.

Set the 12 paper cups in a muffin pan. Fill the cake mixture into a piping bag and fill the paper cups ⅔ full. Bake for 15 minutes (on the middle shelf). Take out and let cool in the pan for 5 minutes, then turn out onto a wire rack to cool.

Cut the gateaux in half horizontally. Drizzle cherry liqueur onto the bottom half. Whip the cream until stiff and beat in the icing/confectioners' sugar. Spread half the cream onto the cake bases and place a couple of cherries on the cream. Place the top half on each cake and top with the remaining cream.

Garnish the gateaux with chocolate shavings and one cherry each. Dust with cinnamon and cocoa to serve.

Cherry cheesecake

Prep and cook time: 2 hours
Can be frozen
Serves: 8-10

Ingredients:
For the pastry:
150 g | 1 ¼ cups plain|all purpose flour
½ tsp baking powder
75 g | ⅓ cup sugar
½ tbsp. vanilla extract
1 pinch of salt
1 egg
75 g | ⅓ cup softened butter
flour, for the work surface

For the filling:
250 g | ¾ cup cherries
3 eggs, separated
200 ml | ⅞ cup cream
750 g | 3 cups quark
(low-fat soft cheese)
150 g | ⅔ cup sugar
2 tsp lemon juice
50 g | ½ cup cornflour|cornstarch
3 - 4 tbsp coconut shavings

Method:

Heat the oven to 200°C (180°C fan) 400°F, gas 6.

For the pastry, mix all the ingredients and work to a smooth dough on a work surface dusted with flour. Roll out and line the springform pan. Bake for 10 minutes, then take out and turn the oven temperature down to 170°C (150°C fan) 350°F, gas 4.

For the filling, beat the egg whites until stiff. Whip the cream until stiff. Mix the egg yolks with the quark, sugar, lemon juice and cornflour/cornstarch. Fold in the beaten egg whites and whipped cream. Finally fold in the cherries and spread evenly on the pre-baked pastry base.

Sprinkle with coconut shavings. Bake for 60 minutes, or until done. Serve cold.

Scones with clotted cream and jam

Prep and cook time: 40 minutes
Cannot be frozen
Makes: 10-12 scones

Ingredients:
225 g | 1 ¾ cups plain|all purpose flour
1 tsp baking powder
1 tsp sugar
50 g | ¼ cup soft butter
150 g yoghurt
1 egg yolk, beaten
150 g | ¾ cup clotted cream
150 g | ½ cup strawberry jam (jelly)

To decorate:
icing|confectioners' sugar

Also needed:
flour, for the worksurface

Method:
Heat the oven to 220°C (200°C fan) 425°F, gas 7.

Knead the flour with the baking powder, sugar, ½ tsp salt and butter, adding enough yoghurt to make the dough smooth and easy to knead.

Roll out the dough on a floured surface to about 2 cm / ¾" thickness. Cut out scones with a fluted pastry cutter (5 cm / 2" diameter). Brush the scones with beaten egg and bake for about 15 minutes until golden brown. Let cool and dust with icing/confectioners' sugar.

Cut in half and serve with clotted cream and jam.

Apple tart with pine nut crumble

Prep and cook time: 1 hour 40 minutes
Cannot be frozen
Serves: 8-10

Ingredients:
For the dough:
125 g | 1 cup plain|all purpose flour
75 g | ³/₈ cup butter
50 g | ¹/₂ cup icing|confectioners' sugar
¹/₂ tsp baking powder
1 egg
1 lemon, grated zest

For the filling:
600 g | 1 ¹/₂ lbs apples, peeled,
cored, quartered
3 tbs lemon juice
20 g | ¹/₄ cup shredded coconut
125 g | 1 cup mascarpone
50 g | ³/₈ cup sugar
1 egg yolk
2 tbsp brown sugar

For the crumble:
50 g | 2 tbsp pine nuts, chopped
50 g | ³/₈ cup sugar
60 g | ¹/₄ cup butter
80 g | ²/₃ cup plain|all purpose flour

To decorate:
icing|confectioners' sugar

Method:
For the dough, mix the flour, butter, icing/confectioners' sugar baking powder, egg and ¹/₂ tsp salt to pastry.
Shape the dough into a ball, wrap in plastic wrap and chill in the fridge for at least 30 minutes.

Slice the apple quarters thinly and drizzle lemon juice over them.

Heat the oven to 200°C (180°C fan) 400°F, gas 6.

Roll out the pastry and line the tart pan with it. Stir the shredded coconut into the mascarpone with the sugar and egg yolk. Spread the mixture onto the pastry base, cover with apple slices and sprinkle with brown sugar.

For the crumble, rub the pine nuts into the sugar, butter and flour. Sprinkle the crumble over the apples and bake the tart for 30 minutes until golden brown.

Dust with icing/confectioners' sugar and serve.

63

Cherry and coconut cake

Prep and cook time: 1 hour 50 minutes
Can be frozen
Serves: 12

Ingredients:

For the sponge:
8 eggs, separated
1 dash lemon juice
200 g | 1 cup sugar
200 g | 1 ⅔ cups plain|all purpose flour
1 tsp baking powder

For the garnish:
200 g | 1 ¾ cups coarsely shredded coconut
100 g | ½ cup candied cherries, chopped
3 tbsp Grenadine

For the cream:
200 g | 1 cup quark (low-fat soft cheese), drained
200 g | 1 cup mascarpone
200 g yoghurt
100 ml | 7 tbsp cream
4 tbsp finely shredded coconut
½ lemon, juice squeezed
100 g | ½ cup candied cherries, chopped
2 tbsp sugar

Method:

Heat the oven to 200°C (180°C fan) 400°F, gas 6.

For the sponge, beat the egg whites with the lemon juice until stiff. Gradually add the sugar while stirring and beat until stiff and glossy.

Beat the egg yolks. Sift the flour with the baking powder. Fold the flour and egg yolks alternately into the egg whites to make a smooth, light mixture.

Butter the base of the pan and dust with flour. Spoon in the dough and bake for 50 minutes. Test with a toothpick, if it comes out clean, the cake is done. If necessary, cover with foil to prevent the cake browning too much.

Let the cake cool in the pan. Then take out and cut through horizontally three times.

For the garnish, mix the coconut with the cherries and the Grenadine. Let soak.

For the cream, mix the quark, mascarpone and yoghurt until smooth. Whip the cream until stiff and fold in. Add the coconut. Stir in the lemon juice with the sugar and the cherries (more sugar may be used if preferred).

Spread half the cream smoothly on three of the four cake bases and set the bases one on top of the other, with the fourth as a lid on top. Press down lightly. Spread the rest of the cream on the top and sides of the cake. Sprinkle with the pink coconut garnish.

Chill for 2 hours before serving.

Toffee pecan pie

Prep and cook time: 1 hour 15 minutes Chilling: 1 hour
Can be frozen
Serves: 8

Ingredients:
For the pastry:
300 g | 2 ½ cups plain|all purpose flour
1 tsp baking powder
100 g | 1 cup quark (low-fat soft cheese)
100 g | ½ cup sugar
1 tsp vanilla extract
100 g | ½ cup butter
1 egg

For the filling:
35 g | ⅛ cup butter
2 tbsp honey
20 ml | 4 tsp water
250 g | 1 ¼ cups sugar
90 ml | ⅜ cup | ½ cup condensed milk
5 tbsp cream
200 g pecan nuts

Method:
Heat the oven to 180°C (160°C fan) 375°F, gas 5.

For the pastry, mix the flour with the baking powder. Sift onto the work surface and make a dip in the middle. Place the quark and the egg into the dip. Sprinkle the sugar, the vanilla extract, a pinch of salt and the butter in small pieces around the dip and knead quickly to pastry. Shape into a ball, wrap in cling film and chill for 1 hour in the fridge.

For the filling, place all ingredients except the cream and pecan nuts into a heavy saucepan and heat over a low heat, stirring continuously until the sugar has dissolved. Turn the heat up, bring to a boil and boil for 12 minutes (the mixture is ready when you can place a spoonful in cold water and shape it into a soft ball with your fingers = 115°C on a sugar thermometer). Let cool until it is only warm.

Roll out ¾ of the pastry on a floured surface. Lay the pastry in the pan, forming a 4 cm / 1½" high rim. Prick several times with a fork, cover with baking parchment weighted with dried beans and bake for 15 minutes. Remove the parchment and beans.

Roast the pecans in a skillet without fat. Chop ¾ of the nuts. Place the chopped nuts in the toffee mixture and beat with the hand mixer until it is thick and creamy. Stir in the cream. Pour at once into the pastry base.

Roll out the remaining pastry to 3-5 mm / ⅛" thick. Roll a multi-wheeled pastry cutter over the pastry and carefully pull the strands apart, or cut thin strips with a knife. Lay the strips over the cake like a grid and sprinkle the remaining pecans in between the pastry strips. Bake for a further 12-15 minutes.

Easter cake with white chocolate scrolls and Easter eggs

Prep and cook time: 1 hour 20 minutes Chilling: 2 hours
Cannot be frozen
Makes: 1 cake (26 cm / 10 ½" diameter)

Ingredients:
100 g | ½ cup butter
120 g | ⅝ cup sugar
5 eggs
150 g | 1 ¼ cups plain|all purpose flour
3 tbsp cocoa
1 tsp baking powder

For the filling:
5 sheets white gelatine
250 g yoghurt
50 g | ¼ cup sugar
1 tsp ground ginger
250 ml | 1 cup cream
1 tbsp lemon juice

Also needed:
150 g white chocolate
candy eggs

Method:
Heat the oven to 200°C (180°C fan) 400°F, gas 6.

Line the pan with baking parchment. Beat the butter until pale and fluffy. Beat in the sugar, then the eggs. Mix the flour, cocoa and baking powder; beat into the egg mixture. Fill the dough into the pan and bake for 30 minutes, allow it to cool. Take out of the pan and cut in half horizontally.

For the filling, soften the gelatine in cold water. Mix the yoghurt with the sugar and ginger. Melt the wet gelatine in a small saucepan over a low heat and stir into the yoghurt cream.

Place a gateau ring around the cake base. Whip the cream with the lemon juice until stiff and mix with the yoghurt cream. Spread ⅔ of the cream mixture onto the cake base and place the second half on top. Spread the remaining cream over the top. Chill for at least 2 hours.

Melt the white chocolate in a bowl over a saucepan of simmering water. Pour onto a board and let cool. Scrape chocolate scrolls with a palette knife. Decorate the cake with the scrolls and candy eggs. A ribbon may be wrapped around the cake.

Raspberry and white chocolate gateau

Prep and cook time: 1 hour 20 minutes
Cannot be frozen
Serves: 8-10

Ingredients:
For the cake:
200 g | 1 ½ cups white chocolate, chopped
200 g | ⅞ cup butter
1 tbsp cherry liqueur
4 eggs, separated
150 g | ¾ cup sugar
80 g | ⅔ cup plain|all purpose flour

To decorate:
150 ml | ⅔ cup cream
200 g | 1 ⅔ cups raspberries
50 g | ⅜ cup white chocolate

Method:

Line the base of the pan with baking parchment and butter the sides. Place the chocolate and the butter in a small bowl. Place over a saucepan of boiling water and let melt. Stir in the cherry liqueur. Take off the heat and let cool.

Heat the oven to 180°C (160°C fan) 375°F, gas 5.

Beat the egg whites until stiff. Beat the yolks with the sugar until pale and creamy. Stir in the cool chocolate butter. Quickly beat in the flour. Stir 2 tbsp egg white into the dough, then carefully fold in the rest.

Place the dough in the pan, smooth the top and bake for 30-40 minutes. Test using a wooden toothpick, if it comes out clean, the cake is done. Let cool in the pan, then take out of the pan and peel off parchment.

Set the cake on a plate. Whip the cream until stiff and spread over the cake. Cover with the raspberries. Scrape shavings or scrolls from the chocolate using a potato peeler and sprinkle them over the cake.

Tarte tatin

Prep and cook time: 1 hour 10 minutes
Cannot be frozen
Serves: 8-10

Ingredients:
For the pastry:
200 g | 1 ³/₈ cups plain|all purpose flour
1 tsp sugar
100 g | ¹/₂ cup cold butter
1 egg

For the filling:
75 g | ⁵/₈ cup butter
200 g | 1 cup sugar
750 g | 1 ³/₄ lbs apples, peeled,
cored and chopped

Method:
Make a mound of flour on the work surface. Mix in a pinch of salt and the sugar. Make a dip in the middle of the flour. Sprinkle small pieces of the cold butter around the dip and break the egg into the dip. Chop everything thoroughly with a knife to form dough crumbs. Knead quickly by hand to a dough, shape to a ball and wrap in plastic wrap.
Chill for 30 minutes.

Butter the pie pan with 50 g / ³/₈ cup of the butter and sprinkle on a thick layer of sugar, 100g / ¹/₂ cup. Arrange the apple slices in layers on the sugar.

Place the pie pan on the cooker at medium heat for about 15 minutes. Remove when the sugar begins to caramelize.
Cool briefly, then sprinkle the remaining sugar over the apple and dot with the remaining butter.

Heat the oven to 220°C (200°C fan) 425°F, gas 7.

Roll out the pastry and lay it on top of the apples. Press the edges down into the pan slightly. Bake the tart for 30 minutes.

Take out and let cool. Turn out onto a large dish and serve.

Mixed berry crumble

Prep and cook time: 40 minutes
Cannot be frozen
Serves: 4

Ingredients:
400 g | 1 lbs mixed berries
125 g | ¼ lbs cherries, pitted
2 tbsp sugar
3 tbsp blackcurrant jam (jelly)
400 ml | 1 ⅔ cassis liqueur
70 g | ⅓ cup plain|all purpose flour
60 g | ⅜ cup sugar
50 g | ¼ cup butter

Method:

Heat the oven to 180°C (160°C fan) 375°F, gas 5.

Mix the fruit with the sugar, blackcurrant jam and liqueur.

Pour into four oven-proof cups or mugs.

Rub the flour, sugar and butter together to make crumble. Sprinkle over the fruit.

Bake for 15 minutes. Remove from oven and serve while still warm with cream or custard.

Cherry pie

Prep and cook time: 1 hour 45 minutes
Can be frozen
Serves: 8

Ingredients:
For the pastry:
250 g | 2 cups plain|all purpose flour
125 g | ⅝ cup cold butter
3 tbsp sugar
1 pinch salt
1-2 tbsp cream

For the filling:
1 lemon, juiced and zest grated
4 tbsp sugar
2 ½ tbsp cornflour|cornstarch
750 g | 1 ¾ pounds Morello
cherries, pitted
2 tbsp dry breadcrumbs
1 egg yolk, beaten

Method:
Put the flour in a bowl and add the butter in small pieces. Knead in the sugar, a pinch of salt and the cream to form a pastry dough, adding 1-2 tbsp cold water if necessary.

Divide the pastry and shape 2 balls. Wrap these in cling film and chill for 1 hour in the fridge.

Mix the lemon juice and zest with the sugar and cornflour/cornstarch, add the cherries and leave for 30 minutes.

Heat the oven to 200°C (180°C fan) 400°F, gas 6.

Roll out the two pastry balls on a floured surface between layers of cling film. Lay the larger circle in the greased pie pan and make a rim. Sprinkle the base with dry breadcrumbs.

Set aside ¼ of the cherry mix and let drain. Catch the liquid and add it to the rest of the cherries. Fill the cherry mixture onto the base and cover lightly with the second pastry circle. Press the edges down firmly. Brush with beaten egg.

Arrange the remaining cherries on the pie and press them gently into the pastry.

Bake the pie for 45-55 minutes. Remove from the oven and allow to cool.

Mocha cheesecake

Prep and cook time: 1 hour 30 minutes
Can be frozen
Serves: 12-16

Ingredients:
1 lemon, juiced, zest finely grated
200 g | good ¾ cup soft butter
200 g | 1 cup sugar
1 vanilla pod, slit open lengthways,
seeds removed and reserved
4 eggs, separated
100 g | 3 ½ oz milk chocolate
750 g | 3 cups quark
(low-fat soft cheese)
1 tbsp cream of semolina | cream
of wheat
4 ½ tbsp cornflour | cornstarch
1 ½ tsp vanilla extract
4 tbsp dark cocoa powder
2 tbsp instant espresso powder
baking parchment
fat, to grease the pan

Method:
Heat the oven to 220°C (200°C fan) 425°F, gas 7. Line a baking pan with baking parchment and lightly grease the sides.

Cream the butter and sugar until light and fluffy. Add the vanilla seeds to the creamed mixture. Add the egg yolks, lemon juice and grated zest and mix thoroughly.

Melt the chocolate over a hot bain marie, then set aside and let cool.

Stir the quark, semolina/cream of wheat, cornflour/cornstarch and vanilla extract into the creamed mixture. Mix ⅓ of the mixture with the chocolate, cocoa powder and espresso powder.

Beat the egg whites until stiff and fold ¼ into the cocoa mixture. Fold the rest into the white mixture.

Spread the mocha mixture in the prepared springform pan, reserving 4 tbsp. Spread the white cream on top. Put the rest of the mocha cream into a freezer bag and snip off one corner. Pipe the mocha mixture on the surface of the cheesecake and marble with a fork.

Bake in the preheated oven for 30-35 minutes (middle shelf), then reduce the temperature to 200°C (180°C fan) 400°F, gas 6 and bake for a further 20-25 minutes. Cover with foil if it browns too quickly.

Cool in the pan.

Chocolate soufflé cupcakes

Prep and cook time: 1 hour
Cannot be frozen
Serves: 8

Ingredients:
4 eggs separated
50 g | ¼ cup butter, softened
50 g | ½ cup flour
250 ml | 1 cup milk
50 g | ⅓ cup milk chocolate, chopped
70 g | ⅓ cup sugar
1 pinch salt

Also:
melted butter to grease the dishes
sugar for sprinkling
icing|confectioners' sugar

Method:

Preheat the oven to 200°C (180°C fan) 400°F, gas mark 6.

Butter 8 soufflé dishes or cups evenly with cooled (almost cold) melted butter and sprinkle with sugar. The base and sides of the dishes should be completely covered. Tip out the excess sugar.

Cut the butter and flour together until well combined.

Pour the milk into a pan, add the chocolate and sugar and bring to the boil, stirring constantly.

Crumble the flour and butter mixture into pieces and stir into the boiling milk little by little, stirring constantly until the flour has thickened the liquid to a smooth consistency.

Let the soufflé batter cool to lukewarm, then whisk in the egg yolks one at a time, whisking until the mixture is smooth and creamy again.

Beat the egg whites with a pinch of salt until they form soft peaks.

Whisk about ¼ of the beaten egg white into the soufflé batter to lighten the mixture. Then fold in the rest of the beaten egg with a wooden spoon.

Fill the prepared dishes or cups with the mixture to 1 cm / ½" below the rim.

Place the dishes in a baking dish and add boiling water to a depth of 1.5 cm / 1 ¼" below the rim of the dishes and bake in the bain marie for 25-30 minutes.

Remove from the oven. Place a paper heart on top of each soufflé and sprinkle with icing/confectioners' sugar. Remove the paper heart and serve immediately.

Strawberry custard

Prep and cook time: 50 minutes
Cannot be frozen
Serves: 4

Ingredients:
250 ml | 1 cup milk
½ vanilla pod, slit open lengthways
50 g | ⅜ cup sugar
2 eggs
1 egg yolk

For the caramel:
50 g | ⅜ cup sugar

Also needed:
4 flan pans
100 g | ¼ lb strawberries, chopped

Method:

Heat the oven to 180°C (160°C fan) 375°F, gas 5.

Boil the milk with the vanilla pod and set aside to cool slightly. Stir the sugar into the eggs and egg yolk very thoroughly, but do not beat until it foams. Then pour the milk in a thin stream into the egg mixture, stirring all the time.

For the caramel, oil the flan pans lightly. Simmer the sugar with 1 tbsp water in a small saucepan until the sugar is golden brown. Pour at once into the flan pans.

Pour the custard mixture into the pans. Fill a large oven-proof dish with 2 cm / ½" in water. Place the flans into the water and bake for 30 minutes. After 10 minutes, place the strawberries on top of the custards before continuing to cook.

Take the custards out and let cool. Run a sharp knife around the rims to loosen the custards and turn out upside down onto plates to serve.

Carrot cake

Prep and cook time: 2 hours
Can be frozen
Serves: 8-10

Ingredients:
For the dough:
6 eggs, separated
250 g | 1 ¼ cups sugar
1 lemon, zest grated
300 g | 2 cups carrots, finely grated
300 g | 2 ½ cups ground hazelnuts
(cob nuts)
100 g | ¾ cup plain|all purpose flour

To decorate:
icing|confectioners' sugar

For the carrots:
200 g | 1 cup marzipan paste
100 g | ¾ cup icing|confectioners'
sugar
food colouring, red and green

Method:

Heat the oven to 200°C (180°C fan) 400°F, gas 6.

Beat the egg yolks with ⅓ of the sugar, a pinch of salt and the lemon zest until pale and creamy. Beat the egg whites until stiff. Gradually add the remaining sugar and continue to beat until very stiff.

Mix the carrot, nuts and flour. Add ⅓ of the egg white to the egg yolk mixture and mix in well. Spoon the remaining egg white on top and sprinkle over the nut mixture. Fold in very carefully, using a wooden spoon.

Line the pan with baking parchment and pour in the dough. Smooth the top and bake for 60 minutes. Allow to cool in the pan overnight.

Turn the cake out onto a sheet of baking parchment, so that the smooth underside is on top. Knead the marzipan paste with the icing/confectioners' sugar until smooth. Colour about ⅙ green, the rest orange (using the red food colouring). Divide into 16 pieces and shape into little carrots with leaves.

Dust the cake with icing sugar and decorate with the carrots.

Chocolate and vanilla custard pie

Prep and cook time: 1 hour 10 minutes Chilling: 4 hours
Cannot be frozen
Serves: 8-10

Ingredients:
For the pastry:
250 g | 2 cups plain|all purpose flour
100 g | ½ cup butter
1 egg

For the chocolate cream:
**300 g | 2 ¼ cups dark chocolate,
a little grated, the rest chopped**
**100 g | ⅝ cup chopped hazelnuts
(cob nuts)**
100 g | ⅓ cup crème fraiche

For the vanilla cream:
5 sheets gelatine
400 ml | 1 ⅔ cognac
250 g | 1 ¼ cup mascarpone
1 tbsp vanilla extract
**150 g | 1 ⅜ cup
icing|confectioners' sugar**
400 ml | 1 ⅔ cups cream

Method:

For the pastry, mix the flour, butter, egg, a pinch of salt and 4 tbsp cold water to a pastry dough. Shape into a ball, wrap in cling film and place in the fridge for 1 hour.

Heat the oven to 180°C (160°C fan) 375°F, gas 5.

Take ⅓ of the pastry and shape it into a long roll. Twist the roll. Roll out the remaining pastry for the base and place in the pie pan. Arrange the twisted roll around the rim and press on firmly. Prick the pastry base several times with a fork. Cover with baking parchment weighted with dry beans and bake for 25 minutes. Remove the beans and parchment and let cool.

For the chocolate cream, melt the chopped chocolate with the créme fraiche in a bowl over a saucepan of simmering water. Stir in the nuts and let cool slightly. Spread onto the pastry base and smooth over the top. Chill for at least 1 hour.

For the vanilla cream, soften the gelatine in cold water and squeeze it out. Warm the cognac and dissolve the gelatine in it.

Stir the mascarpone with the vanilla flavor and 100g / ⅞ cup icing/confectioners' sugar. Whip the cream with the remaining icing/confectioners' sugar until stiff and reserve about ¼ to garnish.

Stir 2 tbsp of the mascarpone cream into the dissolved gelatine and then mix all into the remaining mascarpone cream. Fold in the whipped cream and spread onto the pie base. Smooth the top and pipe on dots with the remaining whipped cream.

Sprinkle with the grated chocolate and let set for at least 2 hours.

Strawberry cake

Prep and cook time: 2 hours
Cannot be frozen
Serves: 8-10

Ingredients:
For the sponge base:
4 eggs, separated
120 g | ⅝ cup sugar
80 g | ⅔ cup plain|all purpose flour
50 g | ⅓ cup cornflour|cornstarch
200 g | ⅔ cup strawberry jam (jelly)

For the vanilla cream:
500 ml | 2 cups milk
1 vanilla pod
5 egg yolks
100 g | ½ cup sugar
30 g | ¼ cup plain|all purpose flour

To garnish:
500 g | 1 lb small strawberries, one quarter chopped into quarters
80 g | 1 cup flaked|slivered almonds

Method:
Heat the oven to 180°C (160°C fan) 375°F, gas 5.

For the sponge base, have all ingredients ready before you start. Grease the base of a loose-bottomed pan. Beat the egg yolks with half the sugar until fluffy. Beat the egg whites until fairly stiff; add the remaining sugar gradually and continue to beat until quite stiff. Fold the egg whites into the egg yolks.

Sieve the flour with the cornflour/cornstarch over the egg mixture and fold in. Spoon the dough into the prepared pan, smooth the top and bake on the middle shelf for 25-30 minutes. Take out, let cool slightly and run a thin knife carefully around the side of the pan to loosen the cake. Turn out onto a wire rack and let cool for at least 2 hours.

For the vanilla cream, slice the vanilla pod lengthways, scrape out the seeds and add the seeds and the pod to the milk. Bring to a boil. Beat the egg yolks with the sugar until creamy; then stir in the flour. Gradually stir the boiling milk into the egg yolk cream; then pour it all back into the saucepan.

Remove the pod and keep stirring over a low heat (do not boil!) until the mixture thickens. Pass the vanilla cream through a sieve and let cool. Sprinkle the surface with sugar to prevent a skin from forming.

Roast the almonds in a pan without fat. Halve the sponge base horizontally. Spread strawberry jam over the lower half. Place the upper half on top. Spread the vanilla cream on top and around the edge; decorate the top with strawberries.

Sprinkle the almonds around the edge of the cake.

Chocolate mousse gateau with rum

Prep and cook time: 1 hour Chilling time: 2 hours
Cannot be frozen
Serves: 8-10

Ingredients:
For the dough:
6 eggs
200 g | 1 cup sugar
200 g | 1 ²/₃ cup plain|all purpose flour
¹/₂ tsp baking powder
50 g cocoa

For the filling:
180 g | 1 ³/₄ cups dark chocolate,
70% cocoa solids, chopped
40 g | ¹/₄ cup butter
1 tbsp brown rum
1 ¹/₂ tsp powdered gelatine
3 eggs, separated
60 g | ¹/₄ cup sugar
100 ml | 7 tbsp whipping cream

To decorate:
chocolate scrolls

Method:

Heat the oven to 200°C (180°C fan) 400°F, gas 6.

For the dough, beat the eggs with the sugar until pale and creamy. Mix the flour, baking powder, cocoa and a pinch of salt. Sift over the egg mixture and fold in carefully.

Line a cookie sheet (30 cm x 40 cm / 12" x 16") with baking parchment. Spread the dough on the cookie sheet and bake for 25 minutes. Turn onto a wire rack and let cool, covered with a cloth. Cut into four pieces.

For the filling, melt the chocolate in a bowl over a saucepan of simmering water. Stir in the butter in small pieces. Add the rum and stir in.

Mix the gelatine with a little cold water and let soak for 10 minutes to soften. Beat the egg yolks with half of the sugar and the gelatine in a bowl over a pan of simmering water until thick and creamy. Let cool slightly and add to the chocolate. Mix well.

Beat the egg whites with a pinch of salt until stiff. Gradually add the remaining sugar. Fold carefully into the chocolate mixture. Beat the double cream for about 2 minutes and stir into the chocolate mixture. Spread the chocolate mixture evenly onto the four cake bases and place them on top of each other.

Chill for 2 hours. Decorate with chocolate scrolls to serve.

Baked Alaska

Prep and cook time: 1 hour 15 minutes Freezing: 12 hours
Cannot be frozen
Serves: 8-10

Ingredients:
For the ice-cream:
250 ml | 1 cup double cream
3 egg yolks
2 tbsp icing|confectioners' sugar
50 ml | ⅕ cup peppermint syrup

For the sponge:
2 eggs, separated
50 g | ¼ cup sugar
50 g | ⅓ cup plain|all purpose flour

For the meringue:
3 egg whites
120 g | ½ cup icing|confectioners' sugar
1 tbsp lime juice, and zest

Method:

For the ice-cream, heat the cream; beat the egg yolks with the icing/confectioners' sugar and a pinch of salt until creamy. Stir in the peppermint syrup. Add the hot cream and beat the mixture in a bowl over a saucepan of simmering water until it thickens slightly. Place the bowl over a pan of cold water and stir until cool. Chill in the fridge for 30 minutes.

Stir the ice-cream again, fill into an ice-cream maker and let freeze for 15 minutes. Or place the ice-cream in a freezing container and freeze in the freezer for 5 hours, beating the mixture several times in the first hour or two.

Place the frozen ice-cream in a bowl (24 cm / 9½" diameter), ensuring there are no air bubbles in it. Freeze overnight.

Heat the oven to 180°C (160°C fan) 375°F, gas 5.

For the sponge, beat the egg whites until stiff. Beat the egg yolks with the sugar and 2 tbsp water until pale and creamy. Sift the flour over the egg yolks and fold in. Fold in the egg white. Fill the sponge mixture into the pan lined with baking parchment and smooth the top. Bake for 12 minutes. Turn out, pull off the parchment and let cool.

For the meringue, beat the egg whites with the lime juice until very stiff. Gradually add the sugar, beating all the time. Fold in the lime zest.

Turn up the oven top heat.

Dip the ice-cream bowl quickly into hot water. Turn the ice-cream out onto the sponge and place on an oven-proof plate. Spoon the meringue mixture over the ice-cream and cook for 5 minutes, until the meringue tips are lightly browned. Serve immediately.

Lemon pie

Prep and cook time: 1 hour 15 minutes Chilling: 1 hour
Cannot be frozen
Serves: 8

Ingredients:
For the pastry:
250 g | 2 cups plain|all purpose flour
vanilla extract
1 egg yolk
125 g | ⁵/₈ cup cold butter

For the filling:
5 egg yolks
50 g | ¼ cup sugar
400 g | 1 ¹/₃ cup sweetened
condensed milk
125 ml | ½ cup lemon juice,
freshly squeezed
1 tsp lemon zest
icing|confectioners' sugar

Method:

Place all pastry ingredients in a bowl and chop thoroughly with a knife. Knead quickly and form the pastry into a ball. Wrap the ball in cling film and chill for 1 hour.

Heat the oven to 180°C (160°C fan) 375°F, gas 5.

Roll out the pastry on a lightly floured surface to a circle slightly larger than the pie pan. Butter the pan and lay the pastry in it, forming a rim. Line with baking parchment and scatter dried beans on top. Bake for 15 minutes. Remove the parchment and beans and let cool.

Reduce the oven temperature to 160°C (140°C fan) 325°F, gas 3.

For the filling, beat the egg yolks with the sugar until pale and creamy. Stir in the condensed milk. Add the lemon zest and juice, mix well and spread on the pastry base.

Bake for 35–40 minutes. Let cool and sprinkle with icing/confectioners' sugar to serve.

Chocolate nut tart

Prep and cook time: 30 minutes
Cannot be frozen
Serves: 8-10

Ingredients:
For the pastry:
200 g | 1 ⅔ cups plain|all purpose flour
½ tsp baking powder
80 g | ⅓ cup icing|confectioners' sugar
100 g | ⅜ cup cold butter
1 egg yolk

For the filling:
150 g | 1 cup dark chocolate,
70% cocoa solids, chopped
150 g | ⅔ cup soft butter
100 g | ¾ cup icing|confectioners'
sugar
6 eggs, separated
75 g | ⅜ cup sugar
75 g | ¾ cup ground hazelnuts
(cog nuts)
100 g | ¾ cup plain|all purpose flour

For the icing:
125 g | ⅞ cup dark chocolate,
70% cocoa solids, chopped
50 ml | 10 tsp milk
50 g cream
100 g | ¼ lb nougat, raw paste

Also needed:
150 g | ½ cup raspberry jam (jelly)
flour, for the work surface

Method:

For the pastry, sift the flour with the baking powder onto the work surface. Make a dip in the middle of the mound. Sprinkle the icing/confectioners' sugar and the butter in small pieces onto the flour and put the egg yolk in the dip. Mix rapidly to a smooth pastry. Wrap in cling film and chill in the fridge for at least 30 minutes.

Heat the oven to 200°C (180°C fan) 400°F, gas 6.

Butter the tart pan.

Roll out the pastry on a floured surface. Lay it in the pan and prick it with a fork. Cover with baking parchment weighted with dried beans and bake for 15 minutes. Remove the parchment and beans.

For the filling, melt the chocolate in a bowl over a saucepan of simmering water. Beat the butter with the icing/confectioners' sugar until pale and creamy. Stir the egg yolks and the melted chocolate gradually into the butter. Beat the egg whites until fairly stiff; gradually add the sugar and continue to beat until stiff. Fold carefully into the chocolate mixture. Finally, fold in the hazelnuts and the flour.

Spread the raspberry jam onto the pastry base. Spread the chocolate mixture on top and smooth the surface. Bake for 50 minutes. If the pastry rim becomes too dark, cover it with aluminium foil.

Take out of the oven and let cool for at least 2 hours. Take out of the pan.

For the icing, heat the chocolate, milk, cream and nougat, stirring continuously. Let cool until lukewarm. Cover the cake with the chocolate. Let it cool completely and serve.

Apple tarts with meringue topping

Prep and cook time: 2 hours
Cannot be frozen
Serves: 4

Ingredients:
For the pastry:
250 g | 2 cups plain|all purpose flour
1 pinch salt
125 g | ⅔ cup cold butter
1 egg
1 tbsp icing|confectioners' sugar

For the filling:
½ vanilla pod
250 ml | 1 cup milk
2 egg yolks
50 g | ¼ cup sugar
1 tbsp flour
1 pinch salt
3 tbsp apple puree
2 tbsp sugar
2 apples, peeled, cored,
quartered and sliced
1 lemon, juice squeezed

For the meringue topping:
3 egg whites
120 g | 1 cup icing|confectioners' sugar

Method:
Heat the oven to 200°C (180°C fan) 400°F, gas 6.

For the pastry, put the flour in a heap on the work surface, mix in the salt and make a well in the centre. Cut the butter into small pieces and scatter around the well, break the egg into the middle, add the icing/confectioners' sugar, add 40 ml lukewarm water and chop with a knife until it has the consistency of breadcrumbs. Quickly knead to a dough with your hands, form into a ball, wrap in cling film and chill for 30 minutes.

For the filling, slit the vanilla pod open lengthwise, scrape out the seeds, stir into the milk with the pod and bring to a boil.

Beat the egg yolks with the sugar until creamy and mix in the flour and the salt. Stir the boiling milk into the egg yolk mixture and return to the pan. Take out the vanilla pod and beat over a low heat until it returns to the boil. Then stir in the apple puree.

Strain through a sieve and leave to cool, sprinkling the surface lightly with sugar to prevent a skin from forming.

Roll the pastry out thinly between 2 layers of plastic wrap and line the greased tins. Sprinkle the apple slices with lemon juice. Lay the apple slices neatly on the pastry, overlapping the slices, and sprinkle with the rest of the sugar. Bake on the lower shelf of the oven for 25 minutes.

For the topping, whisk the egg whites very stiffly, trickling in the icing/confectioners' sugar. Spread the prebaked tarts with the apple custard. Pipe meringue decoratively on top and bake in a hot oven for a further 10 minutes or so until the meringue begins to brown. Serve on plates.

savoury.

Mini puff pastry pizzas with tomatoes and mint

Prep and cook time: 40 minutes
Cannot be frozen
Makes: 4 pizzas

Ingredients:
250 g ½ lb puff pastry,
defrosted if frozen
1 onion, chopped
2 large tomatoes, sliced
1 tbsp parsley, chopped
1 tbsp mint, chopped
olive oil

To garnish:
4 sprigs mint

Method:

Heat the oven to 200°C (180°C fan) 400°F, gas 6.

Roll out the puff pastry sheets. Cut out round pizza bases (15 cm / 6" diameter) and form a small rim.

Lay on a cookie sheet lined with baking parchment.

Arrange the tomato sliced on the pastry. Season with salt and ground black pepper. Sprinkle onions and fresh herbs over the tomatoes. Drizzle a little olive oil over each pizza and bake for 20 minutes until golden brown.

Serve, garnished with mint sprigs.

Vegetable strudel in yoghurt sauce

Prep and cook time: 1 hour 10 minutes
Can be frozen
Serves: 4

Ingredients:
For the strudel:
1 red bell pepper,
seeds removed, sliced
1 onion, cut into wedges
1 courgette|zucchini, chopped
2 cloves garlic, chopped
4 tbsp butter
1 tsp thyme, chopped
100 g | 1 cup feta cheese
300 g | ¾ lb strudel pastry,
defrosted if frozen
4 tbsp dried breadcrumbs

For the yoghurt sauce:
200 ml | ⅞ cup yoghurt
2 tbsp cream
1 clove garlic, chopped
1 tbsp parsley, chopped
lemon juice

For the garnish:
courgette|zucchini, very finely sliced

Method:

Heat the oven to 220°C (200°C fan) 425°F, gas 7.

Fry the bell pepper, onion, courgette/zucchini and garlic gently in 2 tbsp butter for 5 minutes. Season with salt, ground black pepper and thyme. Take off the heat and crumble the feta over the vegetables.

Lay the strudel pastry sheets on top of each other and cut into 4 rectangles of 15 cm x 20 cm / 6" x 8". Melt the remaining butter and brush the pastry with a little of the melted butter. Sprinkle with the breadcrumbs and spoon the filling onto the middle of the rectangles.

Fold the shorter ends over the filling and roll up. Place on a cookie sheet lined with baking parchment and brush with the remaining butter. Bake for 25-30 minutes until golden brown.

For the sauce, stir the cream into the yoghurt until smooth. Add the garlic and parsley to the sauce. Season with lemon juice.

Take the strudels out of the oven, cut in half and serve on the yoghurt sauce. Garnish with very finely sliced courgette/zucchini.

Yorkshire pudding

Prep and cook time: 25 minutes
Can be frozen
Makes: 12 puddings

Ingredients:
120 g | 4 oz | 1 cup plain|all
purpose flour
100 ml | 3 ½ fl oz | 7 tbsp milk
1 egg
3 tbsp oil, tor the pudding pan

Method:

Heat the oven to 220°C (200°C fan) 425°F, gas 7.

Sieve the flour into a bowl with a pinch of salt. Mix 60 ml / ¼ cup water with the egg and add to the flour. Mix to a smooth batter and stir in the milk.

Brush the cups in the pudding pan with oil and heat in the oven for 5 minutes. Take the pan out of the oven and divide the batter evenly between the cups.

Bake the puddings on the middle shelf of the oven for 10-15 minutes until golden brown.

Bacon and onion muffins with sour cream

Prep and cook time: 50 minutes
Can be frozen
Makes: 12 muffins

Ingredients:
200 g | 1 ¼ cup bacon, chopped
1 onion, chopped
300 g | 2 ½ cups plain|all
purpose flour
3 tsp baking powder
½ tsp baking soda
½ tsp salt
2 eggs
125 g | ⅔ cup sour cream
50 ml | 10 tsp milk

To garnish:
2 tbsp fresh chopped parsley
50 g | ⅓ cup sour cream

Method:

Heat the oven to 200°C (180°C fan) 400°F, gas 6.

Fry the bacon gently without fat. Add the onions and fry briefly with the bacon. Drain on kitchen paper.

Mix flour, baking powder, baking soda and salt in a large bowl. Beat the eggs, milk and sour cream thoroughly in a small bowl, then add to the dry ingredients and beat quickly. Add a little more milk if necessary. Stir in the bacon and onion.

Place the paper cases in the muffin pan and fill each with dough. Bake in the oven for 25 minutes until golden brown. Take the pan out of the oven and let cool.

Take the muffins out of the pan and serve, garnished with a spoonful of sour cream, some parsley and a pinch of ground pepper.

Tomato tart with onions, olives and basil

Prep and cook time: 45 minutes
Cannot be frozen
Serves: 6

Ingredients:
500 g | 1 ¼ lbs white onions, sliced in rings
olive oil
400 g | 1 lb filo pastry
400 g | 1 lb mozzarella, sliced
5 tomatoes, sliced
4 tbsp black olives, pitted

To garnish:
14 basil leaves

Method:

Heat the oven to 200°C (180°C fan) 400°F, gas 6.

Heat 3 tbsp olive oil in a saucepan and fry the onions slowly until golden brown. Season with salt and ground pepper.

Line an oiled cookie sheet with filo pastry, placing several layers on top of each other. Lay the mozzarella slices on the pastry. Place the onion rings evenly over the tart.

Spread the tomato slices and olives over the layer of onions. Drizzle 2 tbsp olive oil over. Season with salt and ground black pepper.

Bake for 25-30 minutes until golden brown. Garnish with basil leaves and serve.

Cod on asparagus baked in pastry

Prep and cook time: 35 minutes
Cannot be frozen
Serves: 4

Ingredients:
500 g | 1 ¼ lbs green asparagus
500 g | 1 ¼ lbs white asparagus
1 tbsp mixed peppercorns
2 tbsp freshly chopped herbs,
chives and parsley
250 g | ½ lb brick pastry
(4 sheets 20 cm x 20 cm | 8" x 8")
4 x 160g | 6 oz pieces cod
1 lemon, juiced
2-3 tbsp butter

Method:
Heat the oven to 200°C (180°C fan) 400°F, gas 6.

Peel the lower third of the green and white asparagus. Simmer the white asparagus for 10 minutes in salted water; add the green asparagus and simmer together for a further 5 minutes until almost done. Remove from the water and allow to cool slightly.

Crush the pepper roughly and mix with the herbs.

Spread out the brick pastry sheets. Lay the asparagus in the middle of each sheet, place the fish on top and drizzle the lemon juice over the fish. Season with salt, the chopped herbs and dot with butter. Fold the pastry over the fish, tuck in the ends and tie the edges together.

Bake for 15-20 minutes until golden.

Pastry crackers with potato and mint filling

Prep and cook time: 30 minutes
Cannot be frozen
Serves: 4

Ingredients:
300 g | ¾ lb waxy potatoes
2 tbsp mint, chopped
50 g | ½ cup fresh Parmesan
cheese, grated
1 egg
2 cloves garlic, chopped
2 tbsp butter
300 g | ⅔ lb filo pastry

For the cream:
125 g | ½ cup sour cream
1 tbsp tomato puree
Tabasco

For the garnish:
4 sprigs mint

Method:
Boil the potatoes in their skins in salted water for 25 minutes until soft. Drain, peel and mash. Mix the potatoes with the mint, Parmesan cheese, egg and garlic. Season with salt and ground pepper.

Heat the oven to 220°C (200°C fan) 425°F, gas 7.

Melt the butter. Cut the filo pastry into rectangles 8 cm x 10 cm / 3" x 4" (makes 20) and brush with a little butter. Spread the potato mixture thinly on the rectangles, leaving a 2 cm rim all round. Roll up the pastry pieces along the short sides and squeeze the ends together.

Place the pastry rolls on a cookie sheet with the join downwards. Brush with the remaining butter and bake for 1 2 minutes until golden brown. Turn once while baking.

Mix the sour cream with the tomato puree, salt and a few drops of Tabasco sauce. Season and fill into small bowls.

Serve the crackers with the cream. Garnish with mint sprigs.

Chicken and bacon pie with egg

Prep and cook time: 2 hours 30 minutes Chilling: 12 hours
Cannot be frozen
Makes: 1 pie

Ingredients:

For the pastry:
750 g | 6 cups plain|all purpose flour
1 tsp salt
150 g | 12 tbsp butter
125 g | 8 tbsp lard
flour, for the work surface

For the filling:
650 g | 1 ½ lbs smoked ham, chopped
300 g | ¾ lbs chicken breasts, chopped
2 tbsp brandy
5 hard boiled eggs, peeled
1 egg, beaten

For the tarragon jelly:
5 sheets white gelatine
300 ml | 1 ⅓ cups chicken stock
2 tsp freshly chopped tarragon leaves

Method:

For the pastry, mix the flour with the salt in a mixing bowl. Melt the butter and lard in a saucepan and bring to a boil; then add to the flour and knead to a soft, elastic dough. Place in a bowl, cover and let stand in a warm place.

Butter the loaf pan.

For the filling, mix the ham and chicken with the brandy in a bowl. Season with salt and freshly ground black pepper.

Heat the oven to 220°C (200°C fan) 425°F, gas 7.

Take ⅓ of the pastry and set aside. Roll out the remaining pastry on a lightly-floured surface and line the bottom and sides of the loaf pan. Spoon ⅓ of the filling into the pastry. Arrange the hard-boiled eggs on the filling. Add the remaining filling and smooth the top.

Roll out the reserved pastry as a lid. Brush the edges of the pie with beaten egg, place the lid on top and press down lightly. Cut off any excess pastry. Cut a small hole in the top to let steam escape. Cut small stars, diamond shapes, etc. from the extra pastry. Brush the pastry with the remaining beaten egg, decorate with pastry shapes and brush these with egg as well.

Bake for 30 minutes in the pre-heated oven, then reduce the heat to 175°C (155°C fan) 350°F, gas 4 and bake for a further 1 ¼ hours. If the pastry gets too dark; cover with foil.

For the jelly, soften the gelatine in cold water. Squeeze the water out. Heat 3-4 tbsp chicken stock in a small saucepan and dissolve the gelatine in the stock. Stir in the tarragon and mix in the remaining chicken stock.

Take out the pie and pour the tarragon jelly gradually into the pie through the hole. Place in the fridge overnight and allow to cool.

Cut in slices to serve.

Potato soufflé

Prep and cook time: 1 hour 10 minutes
Cannot be frozen
Serves: 4

Ingredients:
650 g | 1 ³/₄ lbs potatoes
1 onion, chopped
50 g | ¹/₄ cup butter
150 g | 1 ¹/₂ cups quark (low-fat soft cheese)
2 eggs, separated
1 sprig rosemary, leaves plucked and chopped
50 g | ¹/₂ cup Parmesan cheese
nutmeg

For the garnish:
a few rosemary leaves, whole

Method:

Boil the potatoes in salted water for 30 minutes. Drain, peel and mash. Let cool slightly.

Heat the oven to 180°C (160°C fan) 375°F, gas 5.

Fry the onion in the butter until soft. Let cool slightly. Drain the quark thoroughly and place in a bowl.

Mix the egg yolks and chopped rosemary with the potatoes. Stir in the quark, Parmesan, egg yolks and onions. Beat the egg whites until stiff and fold carefully into the mixture. Season with salt, pepper and nutmeg.

Pour the mixture into a buttered soufflé dish and bake on the middle shelf until golden brown. Garnish with rosemary leaves before serving.

Beef fillet en croute with port sauce

Prep and cook time: 1 hour 20 minutes
Cannot be frozen
Serves: 4

Ingredients:
640 g | 1 ½ lbs beef fillet,
cut into 4 pieces
oil, for frying
250 g | 2 ½ cups button mushrooms,
cleaned, finely chopped
1 shallot, finely chopped
2 tbsp crème fraiche
25 g | 1 cup fresh parsley, chopped
2 egg yolks
2 tbsp breadcrumbs
400 g | 1 lb puff pastry,
defrosted if frozen
250 ml | 1 cup beef stock
250 ml | 1 cup ruby port
2 sprigs thyme
1 sprig rosemary
2 tbsp butter

Method:
Heat the oven to 200°C (180°C fan) 400°F, gas 6.

Season the meat with salt and pepper. Heat the oil and brown the meat on all sides.

Heat 2 tbsp oil and sweat the mushrooms and shallot until all the liquid has evaporated. Remove from the heat and mix with the crème fraiche, chopped parsley, 1 egg yolk and the breadcrumbs. Season with salt and pepper.

Roll out the puff pastry and cut out four large and four small circles. Place the pieces of beef fillet on the large circles and put a quarter of the mushroom mixture on top of each piece of beef. Put the small pastry circles on top and pull the edges of the large circles up to meet the small circles. Press together firmly so that the meat and mushrooms are securely enclosed. Prick the top a few times with a fork and brush with egg yolk.

Place on a baking tray lined with baking parchment and bake for 30 minutes, until golden brown.

For the sauce, put the stock into a pan with the port, thyme and rosemary and boil until reduced by about half. Strain through a sieve and stir in the cold butter. Season to taste with salt and pepper.

Cut each portion of beef fillet in half and arrange on warmed plates. Add a little sauce and serve the rest separately.

Ricotta-asparagus quiche

Prep and cook time: 1 hour 15 minutes
Cannot be frozen
Serves: 4

Ingredients:
For the pastry:
300 g | 3 cups plain|all purpose flour
150 g | ²/₃ cup soft butter
1 egg
1 egg yolk
1 tbsp olive oil
salt

For the filling:
500 g | 1 lb green asparagus
salt
400 g | 2 cups Ricotta cheese
3 eggs
100 g | ¹/₂ cup Parmesan cheese,
grated
nutmeg

In addition:
fat, to grease the dish

Method:
Preheat oven to 200°C (180°C fan) 400°F, gas 6.

Combine the flour, butter, egg and egg yolk, 100 ml / ¹/₃ cup water, oil and a little salt and work to a smooth dough. Form into a ball, wrap in foil or cling film and chill for about 30 minutes.

Wash the asparagus, peel the lower third and cut off the ends. Either leave whole or cut into pieces. Cook in boiling salted, water for 3 minutes, then drain, refresh in cold water and drain thoroughly.

For the filling, mix together the Ricotta, eggs and grated Parmesan cheese and season with salt, pepper and nutmeg.

Roll out the pastry to fit the dish. Grease the dish and line with the pastry. Arrange the asparagus attractively in the lined dish, then spread the ricotta mixture on top.

Bake for 20-25 minutes or until golden brown. Cut into slices and serve warm.

Pork pie

Prep and cook time: 1 hour 30 minutes Resting: 30 minutes
Can be frozen
Makes: 8 pies

Ingredients:
For the pastry:
300 g | 2 ½ cups plain|all purpose flour
1 tsp salt
120 g | 10 tbsp cold butter
2 egg yolks

For the filling:
stale bread roll, chopped
125 ml | ½ cup milk
1 onion, chopped
1 clove garlic, chopped
1 tbsp butter
600 g | 1 ½ lbs minced pork
5 tbsp cream
Cayenne pepper
1 pinch lemon zest
2 tbsp sherry

Also needed:
1 egg yolk
flour, for the work surface

Method:

For the dough, mix the flour, salt, butter and egg yolks with 1-2 tbsp cold water and knead quickly to a smooth dough. Chill for 30 minutes.

For the filling, soften the bread in the milk. Fry the onion and garlic gently in the butter; take off the heat. Mix the pork mince with the onion and garlic in a bowl. Squeeze the bread dry, chop, and add to the meat with the cream. Season with salt, pepper, Cayenne, lemon zest and sherry.

Heat the oven to 200°C (180°C fan) 400°F, gas 6.

Divide the pastry into eight pieces. Roll out each piece on a floured surface and cut out a circle from each to line the pie dish, leaving a circle to fit the each pie dish as a lid. Line the pie dishes with baking parchment.

Line each pie dish with a large pastry circle, covering the sides as well. Spoon in the filling, smooth it and top with the pastry lid. Press the edge of the lid down slightly. Prick several times with a fork and brush the lids with egg yolk.

Bake for 35-40 minutes until golden brown.

Savoury muffins with radicchio and pear salad

Prep and cook time: 1 hour 30 minutes
Cannot be frozen
Makes: 12 muffins

Ingredients:
For the muffins:
600 g | 1 ½ lbs waxy potatoes
25 g | 2 tbsp soft butter
2 tbsp dried breadcrumbs
150 g | 1 ½ cups Gorgonzola cheese
50 g | ½ cup Parmesan cheese, grated
50 ml | 10 tsp | ½ cup milk
3 eggs
1 tsp cream of tartar

For the salad:
2 pears
2 radicchio

For the dressing:
5 tbsp sherry vinegar
2 tbsp honey
3 tbsp walnut oil
1 tbsp chervil, chopped

To garnish:
chervil leaves

Method:
Cook the potatoes for 30 minutes in boiling salted water. Peel and mash.

Heat the oven to 200°C (180°C fan) 400°F, gas 6.

Butter the cups in the muffin pan and sprinkle with breadcrumbs.

Crumble the Gorgonzola into the potatoes. Add the Parmesan, milk, eggs and cream of tartar and mix well. Season with salt and black pepper. Spoon dough into the muffin pan and bake for 30 minutes.

For the salad, quarter and core the pears. Slice into thin wedges. Pull off the radicchio leaves. Arrange pears and radicchio on six plates.

For the dressing, mix the vinegar, honey, walnut oil and chervil, season with salt and pepper and drizzle over the salad.

Place two muffins on each plate and serve, garnish with chervil.

Seafood pie

Prep and cook time: 1 hour 15 minutes
Cannot be frozen
Makes: 1 pie (25 x 25 cm / 10 x 10" in diameter)

Ingredients:
500 g | 1 ¼ lbs fish fillets, chopped
200 g | ¾ cup prawns|shrimps,
ready to cook
2 tbsp lemon, juice
300 g | ¾ lb puff pastry,
defrosted if frozen
3 tbsp butter
2 tbsp plain|all purpose flour
250 ml | 1 cup cream
100 g | 1 cup crème fraiche

To garnish:
2 tbsp parsley, chopped

Method:
Heat the oven to 200°C (180°C fan) 400°F, gas 6.

Mix the fish fillets with the prawns/shrimps. Season with salt and ground pepper and drizzle with lemon juice.

Roll out the puff pastry and cut to the enough to line the pie dish and enough for a lid. Butter the pie dish and line with the pastry, forming a rim.

Melt 2 tbsp butter in a saucepan and stir in the flour. Whisk in the cream using an egg whisk. Cook gently for 5 minutes, season with salt and pepper and stir in crème fraiche.

Stir the fish and prawn mixture into the sauce, pour it into the pastry-lined dish and place the pastry lid on top. Fold in the rim. Make patterns on the lid with a fork and press the lid down onto the rim. Brush with the remaining butter and bake for 40 minutes until golden brown.

Divide into four portions to serve. Garnish with parsley.

Herb pie with basil, parsley and pine nuts

Prep and cook time: 55 minutes Chilling time: 1 hour
Cannot be frozen
Makes: 1 pie

Ingredients:
For the pastry:
250 g | 2 cups plain|all purpose flour
1 pinch of salt
125 g | 10 tbsp cold butter
1 egg

For the filling:
25 g | 2 cups chopped basil
50 g | 4 cups chopped parsley
3 shallots
1 clove garlic
3 tbsp butter
250 g | 1 cup cream
4 eggs
50 g | 2 tbsp pine nuts

To garnish:
basil and parsley

Method:
Place the flour in a heap on a work surface, mix in the salt and make a depression in the middle of the flour. Cut the cold butter into small pieces, scatter around the depression and break the egg into the middle.

Chop with a knife until they have the consistency of breadcrumbs, then quickly knead to a dough using your hands.

Line the greased springform pan with the pastry, forming a rim about 3 centimetres high. Prick the base several times with a fork and chill for 60 minutes.

Wash the basil and parsley, shake dry and chop. Peel and finely chop the shallots and garlic.

Sweat the shallots, herbs and garlic in butter over a low heat, stirring frequently, until the shallots are translucent. Transfer to a dish and leave to cool.

Place the pastry case in a cold oven (middle shelf), set the oven to 200°C (180° fan) 400°F, gas 6 and bake for 15-20 minutes.

Whisk the cream with the eggs and season with salt and pepper. Take the pastry case out of the oven, spread with the herb mixture and scatter with pine nuts. Pour the egg and cream mixture over and return to the oven at a temperature of 180°C (160° fan) 375°F, gas 5 for a further 20 - 25 minutes, or until done.

Cool on a wire rack and garnish with basil and parsley leaves to serve.

Toad in the hole

Prep and cook time: 50 minutes
Cannot be frozen
Serves: 4

Ingredients:
125 g | 1 cup plain|all purpose flour
¹/₂ tsp baking powder
¹/₂ tsp salt
2 eggs
300 ml | 1 ¹/₃ cups milk
500 g | 1 ¹/₄ lbs pork sausages
2 tbsp lard

Method:

Preheat the oven to 200°C (180°C in a fan oven) 400°F, Gas 6.

For the Yorkshire pudding batter, mix the flour, baking powder and salt in a bowl. Add the eggs and milk and mix well. Let the batter stand for 20 minutes.

Put the lard in a roasting tin (15 cm x 30 cm / 6" x 12") and place in the preheated oven.

Prick the sausages a few times. Pour the batter carefully into the roasting tin and place the sausages on top. Bake for 20 minutes, or until golden brown. The Yorkshire pudding should be light and moist, but with a crisp crust.

Spinach and feta parcels

Prep and cook time: 1 hour
Cannot be frozen
Serves: 4 (12 parcels)

Ingredients:
400 g | 1 lb spinach, washed
2 tbsp pine nuts
1 onion, chopped
1 clove garlic, chopped
3 tbsp olive oil
150 g | 1 ¼ cup feta cheese, chopped
2 tsp basil, finely chopped
400 g | 1 lb pastry, defrosted

Method:

Boil the wet spinach in very little water until it wilts; drain. Rinse quickly with cold water. Press out the water and chop.

Roast the pine nuts in a skillet without fat. Fry the onion and garlic in 1 tbsp oil and let cool.

Mix the feta cheese with the spinach, onion and garlic, pine nuts and basil. Season with salt and ground black pepper.

Heat the oven to 200°C (180°C fan) 400°F, gas 6
Line a cookie sheet with baking parchment.

Roll out the pastry thinly and cut into squares 12 cm x 12 cm / 4" x 4". Spoon the filling into the middle of the squares. Fold the squares diagonally over the filling and press the edges down well (you can brush the edges with water so they stick better). Place the parcels on the cookie sheet.

Brush with the remaining olive oil and bake for 25 minutes until golden brown.

Salmon strudel with white wine sauce

Prep and cook time: 1 hour 45 minutes
Cannot be frozen
Serves: 4

Ingredients:
For the strudel pastry:
200 g | 1 ½ cups plain|all purpose flour
1 pinch salt
2 tsp sunflower oil
2 tbsp butter, melted

For the filling:
200 g | ½ lb ready to cook trout fillet, chopped, slightly frozen
2 leaves white cabbage
4 medium kohlrabi (German turnip)
1 egg white
100 ml | 7 tbsp | ½ cup cream
500 g | 1 ¼ lbs salmon fillet
1 egg yolk, beaten

For the sauce:
1 shallot, chopped
1 tbsp butter
150 ml | ⅔ cup white wine
100 ml | 7 tbsp cream
4 tbsp chives, chopped

Method:
For the pastry, mix the flour with the salt and oil.
Add 70-80 ml / ⅓ cup warm water and knead to a fairly firm dough with the kneading hook of the mixer. Turn the dough out onto a worksurface and knead by hand for 10 minutes until smooth and glossy. Cover and let stand.

For the filling, flatten the thick stalk of the cabbage leaves and blanch for 3 minutes in salted water until soft. Dip quickly into cold water and pat dry. Slice one kohlrabi very thinly; halve the other three and slice into 3 mm / ⅛ in thick slices. Blanch the thin kohlrabi slices very briefly, the thicker slices for 2 minutes, so they are still firm. Dip quickly into cold water and pat dry.

Puree the trout finely in a blender. Gradually add the cream and finally the egg white to the trout in the blender. Season with salt and white pepper.

Slice the salmon into 3 cm / 1" wide and 1 ½ cm / ¾" thick strips.

Heat the oven to 200°C (180°C fan) 400°F, gas 6.

Roll out the dough on a lightly floured worksurface and stretch it with the backs of your hands and your fingertips until it is as thin as possible (25 cm x 40 cm / 10" x 16"). Line with the filling lengthways: lay the very thin kohlrabi slices, overlapping slightly, on the first third (leaving a narrow rim). Lay the cabbage leaves and spread the pureed trout on top. Finally add the thicker kohlrabi slices. Place the salmon strips in the middle.

Fold in the short sides and roll the pastry up firmly from the bottom. Place on a cookie sheet lined with baking parchment, brush with beaten egg yolk and bake for 40 minutes until golden brown. Brush with the melted butter occasionally during the cooking time.

For the sauce, fry the shallot gently in butter. Add the white wine and boil until reduced to about half. Add the cream, bring to a boil and puree with a hand blender. Season with salt.

Sprinkle the chives around the rims of the plates. Pour the sauce into the middle and place a piece of strudel on each plate.

Parmesan and pesto muffins

Prep and cook time: 45 minutes
Can be frozen
Makes: 12 muffins

Ingredients:
300 g | 2 ½ cups plain|all purpose flour
½ tsp salt
2 tsp baking powder
150 g | 1 ½ cups Parmesan
cheese, grated
5 tbsp olive oil
20 g basil leaves
2 tbsp pine nuts
300 ml | 1 ⅓ cups buttermilk
1 egg

Method:
Heat the oven to 200°C (180° fan) 400°F, gas 6. Set the paper baking cases in the cups in the muffin pan.

Mix the flour with the salt, baking powder and cheese. Puree the oil with the basil leaves and pine nuts. Stir in the buttermilk and egg. Beat in the flour mixture quickly and spoon the dough into the baking cases.

Bake for 30 minutes. Take out of the oven and let cool slightly, then take the muffins out of the pan and let cool completely.

bread.

Olive bread

Prep and cook time: 1 hour Resting: 4 hours 45 minutes
Can be frozen
Makes: 1 large loaf or 2 small

Ingredients:
450 g | 3 ½ cups plain|all purpose flour
50 g | ⅓ cup whole-wheat flour
100 g | ½ cup coarse wheatmeal
8 ½ g | 1 ½ tsp easy bake yeast
3 - 4 tbsp olive oil
½ tsp oregano
150 - 200 g | 2 cups olives, pitted
(black or green)

Method:

Sieve both types of flour into a bowl. Mix in the coarse wheatmeal, reserving 1 tbsp. Sprinkle the yeast over the flour. Add 300 ml / 1 ¼ cup lukewarm water, 2-3 tbsp olive oil, 1 tsp salt and the oregano. Knead thoroughly.

Shape the dough into one large or two smaller balls. Cover with cling film and let rest for 4 hours.

Heat the oven to 240°C (220°C fan) 475°F, gas 9.

Knead in the olives and shape into one or two loaves. Let rise for a further 45 minutes.

Brush the loaves with the remaining oil and sprinkle with the remaining coarse wheatmeal. Bake for 10 minutes; then reduce the temperature to 200°C (180° fan) 400°F, gas 6 and bake for a further 15-20 minutes.

A large loaf requires 15 minutes longer in the oven.

Salted soft pretzels

Prep and cook time: 50 minutes Rising: 45 minutes
Cannot be frozen
Makes: 2 pretzels

Ingredients:
300 g | 2 ¹⁄₃ cups plain|all purpose flour
4 g | ½ tsp easy bake yeast
1 tbsp soy oil
100 ml | 7 tbsp lukewarm milk
flour, for the work surface
1 egg yolk
1 tbsp coarse salt

Method:

Sift the flour into a bowl and add the yeast and salt. Mix thoroughly. Add the oil, milk and 125 ml / ²⁄₃ cup water and knead with the kneading hook of the electric mixer to a fairly firm dough, which does not stick to the bowl. Cover with a clean cloth and let rise in a warm place until the dough has doubled in size.

Knead the dough once more. Divide it into 2 portions and roll out each portion on a floured surface to a roll as thick as your finger. Form the rolls into pretzel shapes and press the ends down firmly.

Place the dough pretzels on a cookie sheet lined with baking parchment and cover with a clean cloth. Let them rise for about 10 minutes.

Heat the oven to 220°C (200°C fan) 425°F, gas 7.

Beat the egg yolk with 1 tbsp water. Brush the pretzels with egg yolk and sprinkle with coarse salt. Bake on the middle shelf for 20 minutes. Test with a wooden toothpick, if it comes out clean, the pretzels are done.

Cool on a wire rack. Eat while really fresh.

Herb rolls

Prep and cook time: 50 minutes Rising: 1 hour 15 minutes
Can be frozen
Makes: 12 rolls

Ingredients:
50 g | ⅓ cup bacon, cubed
10 stinging nettles, chopped leaves
10 stalks coriander|cilantro,
chopped leaves
4 stalks basil, chopped leaves
2 spring onions|scallions, chopped
7 g | 1 tsp easy bake yeast
1 tbsp salt
250 g | 2 cups rye flour
200 g | 1 ⅜ cups coarse rye flour
150 g dry sourdough
olive oil
flour, for the work surface

Method:

Fry the bacon gently in 1 tbsp oil. Add herbs and spring onions/scallions and fry briefly. Let cool.

Sprinkle the yeast and salt over the two types of flour and the sourdough. Mix in 500 ml / 16 fl oz / 2 cups lukewarm water, the bacon and herbs. Knead to a smooth dough.
Cover and let rise for 30 minutes.

Heat the oven to 240°C (220°C fan) 475°F, gas 9.

Brush the cookie sheet with oil. Turn the dough out onto a floured surface and shape to a roll. Divide the roll into 12 pieces and shape each into a mini loaf, making a slit in the top.
Place on the cookie sheet and let rise for a further 15 minutes.

Brush the rolls with water and place them in the oven (with a bowl of boiling water). Bake for 10 minutes. Reduce the temperature to 180°C (160°C fan) 375°F, gas 5. Brush the rolls with water again and bake for a further 20 minutes.
Cool on a wire rack.

Macadamia and chestnut bread

Prep and cook time: 1 hour 20 minutes Rising: 3 hours 30 minutes
Can be frozen
Makes: 1 loaf

Ingredients:
8 ½ g | 1 ¼ tsp easy bake yeast
½ tsp salt
500 g | 4 cups plain|all purpose flour
150 g | 1 ¼ cups salted macadamia
nuts, chopped (reserve 2 tbsp,
chop finely)
100 g | ⅞ cup chestnut flour
50 ml | 10 tsp oil
2 tsp wheat gluten

Method:

Sprinkle the yeast and salt onto the flour. Mix in 300 ml / 1 ¼ cups lukewarm water. Add the macadamia nuts (reserving 2 tbsp), chestnut flour and oil and knead to a smooth dough. Shape the dough to a ball, cover with a damp cloth and let rise for 3 hours in a warm place.

Knead the dough again briefly. Brush the loaf pan with oil and sprinkle with flour. Fill in the dough and smooth the surface. Cover again and let rise in a warm place for 30 minutes.

Heat the oven to 220°C (200°C fan) 425°F, gas 7.

Place an oven-proof bowl of boiling water in the oven. Put in the bread and bake for 50 minutes. Take out, brush with a little water and sprinkle on the reserved macadamia nuts. Return the loaf to the oven and bake for a further 10 minutes.

Turn the bread out onto a wire rack and let cool completely.

Portuguese bread stuffed with chorizo

Prep and cook time: 1 hour Rising: 1 hour
Can be frozen
Serves: 8-10

Ingredients:
8 ½ g | 1 ¼ tsp easy bake yeast
400 g | 3 ¼ cups plain|all purpose flour
200 g 1 ½ cups cornmeal
1 tsp salt
200 g | ½ lb chorizo, chopped
flour, for the work surface

Method:

Sprinkle the yeast on the two types of flour. Mix in the salt and 350 ml / 1 ½ cups lukewarm water. Knead thoroughly with the kneading hook of the electric mixer, cover and let rise for 30 minutes in a warm place.

Knead the dough on a floured surface. Add either more water or flour if required. Work in the chorizo. Shape the dough to a round loaf and place in the buttered pan. Let rise for a further 30 minutes.

Heat the oven to 220°C (200°C fan) 425°F, gas 7.

Place an oven-proof dish of boiling water in the oven.
Bake the loaf for 30 minutes. Take the bowl of boiling water out after 15 minutes.

Turn the bread out onto a wire rack and let cool completely. Slice to serve.

Sunflower seed bread

Prep and cook time: 1 hour 25 minutes Rising: 1 hour
Can be frozen
Makes: 1 loaf

Ingredients:
14 g | 2 tsp easy bake yeast
1000 g | 8 cups whole wheat flour
1 tsp salt
3 tbsp sunflower oil
50 g ½ cup sunflower seeds

Method:
Sprinkle the yeast onto the flour with the salt. Mix in 500 ml / 2 cups lukewarm water and the oil. Knead to a smooth dough with the kneading hook of the electric mixer. Add more lukewarm water or flour if necessary. Cover and let rise in a warm place for 40 minutes.

Knead the dough on a floured surface, working in the sunflower seeds (reserving 2 tbsp).

Heat the oven to 220°C (200°C fan) 425°F, gas 7.

Shape the dough to a large loaf and place on a cookie sheet lined with baking parchment. Sprinkle with the reserved sunflower seeds. Let rise for a further 20 minutes.

Bake the loaf for 60 minutes. The bread is cooked if it sounds hollow when knocked on the bottom with your knuckle.

Chapatis with dip

Prep and cook time: 40 minutes Rising: 1 hour
Cannot be frozen
Serves: 4

Ingredients:
For the chapatis:
300 g | 2 ½ cups plain|all purpose flour
1-2 tbsp ghee (clarified butter)

For the dip:
5 red bell peppers, halved, seeds
and white skin removed
1 chilli pepper, chopped
1 shallot, chopped
2 cloves garlic, chopped
2 tbsp olive oil
1 lemon, juiced

Method:

For the chapatis, put the flour in a bowl and gradually knead in 150 ml / ⅔ cup water. Turn the dough out onto a lightly floured surface and knead for a further 10 minutes until soft (use a little more or less water if necessary). Wrap the dough in plastic wrap and let rest for 1 hour.

Shape the dough to a roll and divide into 12 pieces. Roll out each piece on a lightly floured surface to thin chapatis of 15 cm / 6" diameter.

Brush a skillet with a little ghee and bake the chapatis at medium heat for 2 minutes on each side, until small brown spots appear. Continue until all chapatis are baked.

For the dip, line a cookie sheet with baking parchment. Lay the bell pepper halves on the cookie sheet, skin side up, and grill for 15 minutes until the skin blisters and starts to turn black. Take out of the oven, cover with a damp cloth and let cool.

Peel the bell pepper halves and chop the flesh. Mix in the chilli pepper, shallot and garlic. Add the olive oil and lemon juice and mix thoroughly.

Irish soda bread

Prep and cook time: 1 hour
Can be frozen
Makes: 1 loaf

Ingredients:
225 g | 1 ¾ cups plain|all purpose flour
225 g | 1 ½ cups whole wheat flour
½ tsp salt
2 tsp baking soda
2 tsp baking powder
3 tbsp soft butter
1 tsp sugar
2 tbsp raisins
350 ml | 1 ½ cups buttermilk
flour, for kneading and dusting

Method:

Preheat the oven to 190°C (170°C fan) 375°F, gas 5.

Line a cookie sheet with baking parchment.

Sieve both flours into a bowl and mix in the salt, baking soda and baking powder.

Rub the butter into the dry ingredients until the mixture resembles breadcrumbs. Then stir in the sugar, raisins and buttermilk to produce a soft dough.

Knead briefly and shape into a round loaf. Place on the prepared baking tray and cut a deep cross in the top of the loaf. Dust the bread lightly with flour.

Stand a bowl of water on the floor of the oven and bake the bread for 35 to 45 minutes. Test to see if it is ready by tapping the underside of the loaf - it will sound hollow when the bread is done. Let cool before slicing.

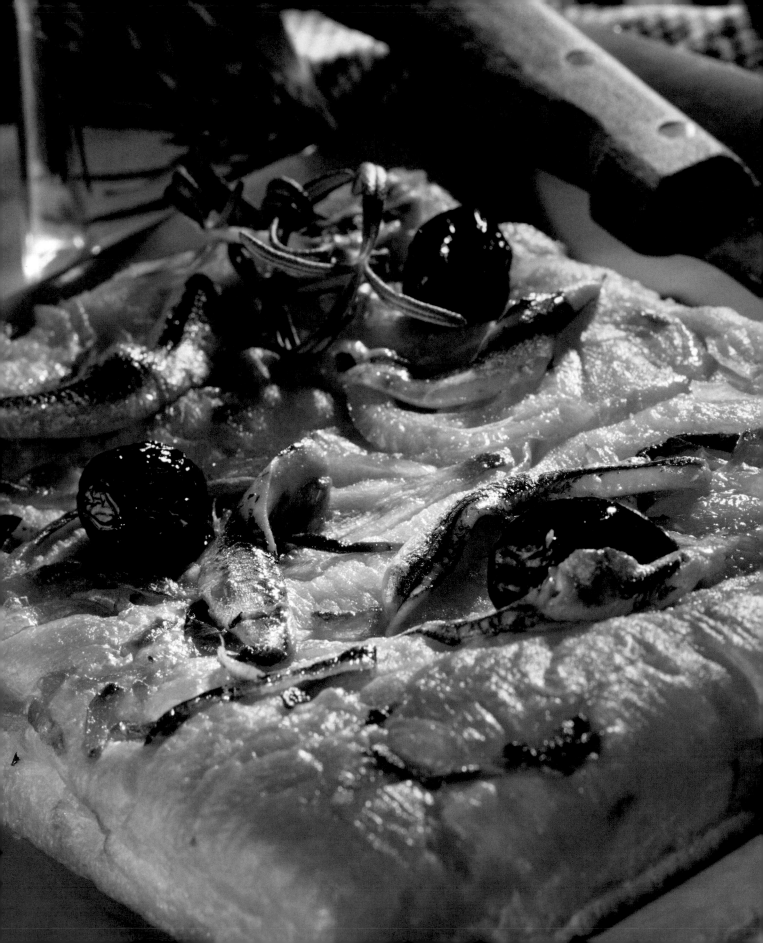

Focaccia with anchovies and olives

Prep and cook time: 40 minutes Rising: 1 hour
Cannot be frozen
Serves: 4-6

Ingredients:
For the dough:
6 g | 1 tsp easy bake yeast
400 g | 3 ¼ cups plain|all purpose flour
½ tsp salt
50 ml | 10 tsp | ¼ cup olive oil
1 tbsp rosemary, chopped
40 g | ⅜ cup small anchovy fillets
40 g | ¼ black olives, pitted
2 tbsp olive oil

Also needed:
flour, for the worksurface
coarse sea salt

Method:

Mix the yeast with the flour and salt in a bowl. Add 200 ml / ⅞ cup lukewarm water and the olive oil. Knead to a smooth dough with the kneading hook of the electric mixer. Cover and let rise in a warm place for 45 minutes.

Heat the oven to 220°C (200°C) 425°F, gas 7.

Knead the dough thoroughly on a floured surface, working in the rosemary. Roll out to form a square flat base (30 cm x 30 cm / 12" x 12"). Cut into 9 small squares.

Place onto a buttered cookie sheet, brush with olive oil and sprinkle with a little coarse sea salt. Lay the anchovies and olives on the dough bases, cover and let rise for a further 15 minutes.

Bake for 30 minutes.

Garlic bread

Prep and cook time: 2 hours 15 minutes
Can be frozen
Makes: 2 loaves

Ingredients:
500 g | 4 cups plain|all purpose flour
100 g | ⅔ cup whole wheat flour
3 tbsp olive oil
1 tsp salt
8 g | 2 tsp easy bake yeast
flour, for the working surface

In addition:
4 tbsp olive oil
pressed garlic
chopped parsley

Method:

Heat the oven to 240°C (220°C fan) 450°F, gas 8.

Put the all purpose flour into a bowl. Reserve 1 tbsp of the whole wheat flour and mix the rest with 2 tbsp oil, the salt and the other flour.

Sprinkle the yeast over the flour. Add 300 ml / 1 ¼ cups lukewarm water and mix. Knead to a smooth dough using the dough hook of the food mixer, cover and put to rise in a warm place for 45 minutes.

Knead thoroughly on a floured working surface, form into 2 balls and let rise for 45 minutes.

Form the balls of dough into longish loaves, brush with the remaining oil and sprinkle with the reserved whole wheat flour.

Bake for 10 minutes, then turn the oven down to 200°C (180°C fan) 400°F, gas 6 and cook for a further 15 - 20 minutes. Take out and let cool.

In a jar, shake the olive oil and crushed garlic together vigorously.

To serve, cut into pieces, drizzle with garlic oil and sprinkle with chopped parsley.

Rosemary potato bread

Prep and cook time: 2 hours 40 minutes
Can be frozen
Makes: 12 bread rolls

Ingredients:
For the dough:
400 g | 3 ¼ cups plain|all purpose flour
5 ½ g | 1 ½ tsp easy bake yeast
2 tbsp olive oil
1 tbsp rosemary leaves, chopped

For the topping:
200 g | ½ lb firm potatoes,
sliced very thinly
2 tbsp olive oil
1 tbsp fresh rosemary leaves

Method:
Pile the flour onto a worksurface; sprinkle on the yeast, a pinch of salt, the oil and rosemary. Make a well in the centre and pour in 325 ml / 1 ½ cups lukewarm water (you may need a little less or more). Knead very thoroughly to a smooth dough. Place in a bowl and let rise for 30 minutes in a warm place, until it has doubled in size.

Heat the oven to 220°C (200°C fan) 425°F, gas 7.

Knead the dough again thoroughly on a floured surface. Shape the dough into 12 balls and flatten them slightly.

Blanch the potato slices for 1-2 minutes. Dip quickly into cold water and drain. Place the potato slices on top of the rolls and press down slightly. Brush with olive oil and sprinkle rosemary leaves on top. Season with salt and pepper.

Place the rosemary potato bread rolls on an oiled cookie sheet and bake for 20-25 minutes until golden brown.

Mushroom flatbread

Prep and cook time: 40 minutes Rising: 45 minutes
Serves: 4

Ingredients:
20 g |$^1/_2$ **cube fresh yeast**
1 **pinch sugar**
250 g | 2 $^1/_2$ **cups plain|all purpose flour**
salt
butter, to grease the baking tray

For the topping:
150 g | 1 $^1/_2$ **cups goat's cheese**
150 g | 1 $^1/_4$ **button mushrooms**
2 **shallots**
olive oil
50 g | 2 **cups rocket|arugula**

Method:

For the dough, put the yeast into a large bowl with 120 ml / $^1/_2$ cup warm water and the sugar and mix smoothly. Then add the flour and salt and knead well until the dough is no longer sticky. Cover with a tea towel and put to rise in a warm place for 45 minutes, by which time it should have doubled in volume.

Preheat the oven to 220°C (200°fan) 425°F, gas 7.

Knead the dough again (not too vigorously) on a floured work surface, then roll out thinly into 1 or 2 flatbreads and put on a greased cookie sheet.

Thinly slice the goat's cheese and spread over the dough, then bake in the hot oven for 15 minutes.

Clean and slice the mushrooms. Peel and thinly slice the shallots. Heat 2 tablespoons olive oil and quickly sauté the mushrooms and shallots over a fairly high heat. Season with salt and pepper and remove from the heat.

Take the flatbread out of the oven, scatter evenly with the mushrooms, shallots and rocket/arugula and served sprinkled with a little olive oil.

Pizza margherita

Prep and cook time: 45 minutes Rising: 1 hour
Can be frozen
Serves: 4

Ingredients:
For the dough:
7 g / 1 ½ tsp easy bake yeast
1 pinch sugar
450 g 3 ½ cups plain|all purpose flour
4 tbsp olive oil
1 tsp salt

For the topping:
1000 g / 2 lbs ripe tomatoes
300 g / 3 cups mozzarella, sliced
1 tsp dried thyme
4 tbsp olive oil
20 g / 1 cup basil

Method:
For the dough, sprinkle the yeast over the flour in a bowl and mix with sugar and 200 ml / ¾ cup of lukewarm water. You may need more water if the dough looks dry. Add olive oil and salt and knead to a smooth dough. Cover and let rise in a warm place for 1 hour.

Heat the oven to 220°C (200°C fan) 425°F, gas 7.

Divide the dough into 4 balls. Roll out the balls on a lightly floured surface to form pizza bases of 22 cm / 9" diameter, with slightly thicker edges. Lay the bases on 4 oiled cookie sheets.

Pour boiling water over the tomatoes, dip them into cold water, peel and chop them. Season with salt and ground pepper and spread over the pizza bases. Place the mozzarella slices on the tomatoes. Sprinkle with thyme and drizzle a little olive oil over the pizzas.

Bake for 25 minutes until golden brown. Garnish with fresh basil leaves and serve.

Calzone with ham and mozzarella filling

Prep and cook time: 1 hour 40 minutes
Can be frozen
Serves: 4

Ingredients:
For the dough:
7 g | 1 tsp easy bake yeast
1 pinch sugar
450 g | 3 ½ cups plain|all purpose flour
3 tbsp olive oil
1 tsp salt
flour, for the work surface

For the filling:
2 onions, chopped
1 clove garlic, chopped
1 tbsp olive oil
400 g | 1 ¼ cups chopped tomatoes
Cayenne pepper
3 tbsp tomato puree
100 g | 1 ½ cups peas, frozen
250 g | 2 ½ cups mozzarella, chopped
200 g | ½ lb cooked
ham, chopped
2 tbsp fresh basil, chopped

Method:

For the dough, sprinkle the yeast over the flour. Add 200 ml / ¾ cup lukewarm water and the other dough ingredients and knead to a smooth dough with the dough hook of the electric mixer; you may need to add more water if the dough looks dry.

For the filling, heat the oil in a large saucepan. Fry the onions and garlic until soft. Add the tomatoes, season with salt, freshly ground black pepper, Cayenne pepper and tomato puree and simmer for about 20 minutes, uncovered, stirring occasionally.

Place the peas in a sieve, rinse with warm water and allow to drain.

Preheat the oven to 220°C (200°C fan) 425°F, gas 7.

Knead the dough once more on a lightly floured surface. Divide into 4 portions and roll each to a circle of 22 cm / 9" diameter. Place some of the tomato sauce, cheese, ham, basil and a few peas on each circle. Fold in half and press the edges firmly.

Place the calzone on a cookie sheet lined with baking parchment and bake for 35 minutes.

Banana nut bread

Prep and cook time: 2 hours
Can be frozen
Makes: 1 loaf

Ingredients:
700 g | 1 ½ lb bananas, chopped
1 lime, juice squeezed
140 g | ⅔ cup sugar
25 g | 2 tbsp butter
2 eggs
250 g | 2 cups plain|all purpose flour
2 tsp baking powder
1 tsp cinnamon
100 g | ¾ cup walnuts, chopped

Method:
Heat the oven to 180°C (160°C fan) 375°F, gas 5.

Puree the bananas with the lime juice. Butter a loaf pan.

Mix the sugar with the butter, eggs and banana puree in a large bowl. Mix the flour, baking powder and cinnamon and stir into the banana mixture, a little at a time. Finally, stir in the nuts.

Place the dough in the pan and bake for 1 hour 10 minutes. Cover with foil after 45 minutes.

Take the cake out and let cool slightly in the pan. Then turn it out onto a rack and let cool completely.

Hot cross buns

Prep and cook time: 2 hours 50 minutes
Can be frozen
Makes: 10 buns

Ingredients:
7 g | 1 tsp easy bake yeast
500 g | 4 cups plain|all purpose flour
1 tsp salt
¼ tsp cinnamon
¼ tsp grated cloves
¼ tsp allspice
50 g | ¼ cup sugar
50 g | ⅓ cup currants
25 g candied orange peel
25 g candied lemon peel
50 g butter, melted
1 egg
125 ml | ½ cup milk, lukewarm

For the cross:
30 g | ¼ cup plain|all purpose flour
40 g | ⅓ cup icing|confectioners' sugar

For the glaze:
4 tbsp sugar

Method:

Sprinkle the yeast over the flour in a mixing bowl. Mix in salt, cinnamon, cloves and allspice. Add 50 g / ¼ cup sugar, currents and candied orange and lemon peel and mix well.

Make a well in the centre of the flour mixture and pour in 125 ml / ⅝ cup lukewarm water and the melted butter. Add the egg and knead, gradually adding the milk, to a firm, smooth dough which forms bubbles. Cover and let rise in a warm place for 1 hour.

Knead the dough again briefly. Shape to a long roll on a floured surface and divide into 10 equal pieces. Form each piece to a ball, flatten slightly with the hand and place on a cookie sheet lined with baking parchment.

Cover with a cloth and let rise for a further 45 minutes. Then press a cross shape into each with a blunt knife.

Heat the oven to 220°C (200°C fan) 425°F, gas 7.

For the cross, mix the flour, icing/confectioners' sugar and 3 tbsp water to a thick paste. Fill the paste into an icing bag with a long nozzle and make cross shapes on the buns where marked. Bake the buns for 20-25 minutes until golden brown.

For the glaze, heat the sugar in 4 tbsp water until it dissolves. Spread over the buns and serve when slightly cooled.

Sweet almond bread

Prep and cook time: 1 hour Rising: 1 hour
Can be frozen
Makes: 1 loaf

Ingredients:
200 g | 1 cup quark
(low-fat soft cheese)
100 ml | 7 tbsp milk
2 eggs
6 tbsp oil
80 g | ⅓ cup sugar
1 tsp lemon zest
300 g | 2 ½ cups plain|all purpose flour
1 tsp baking powder
extra flour, for working

For the filling:
200 g | 1 ¾ cups ground almonds
50 g | ⅓ cup sugar
1 egg white
4 tbsp milk

Also needed:
1 egg yolk

Method:
Mix the quark with the milk, eggs, oil, sugar and lemon zest. Stir in half the flour. Mix the rest of the flour with the baking powder and knead into the dough. The dough should be smooth and firm, not sticky (use a little more or less milk if necessary). Let rise for 45 minutes.

Heat the oven to 180°C (160°C fan) 375°F, gas 5.

Knead the dough thoroughly again and roll out on a well-floured surface to a square of 35 cm x 35 cm / 14" x 14".

Mix the almonds, sugar, egg while and milk to a paste.

Spread the paste on the dough and roll up the dough. Place on a cookie sheet lined with baking parchment and brush with egg yolk. Cut 1 cm / ½" deep zigzags into the loaf and let rise for a further 15 minutes.

Bake for 45 minutes until golden brown. Allow to cool and serve in slices.

Cinnamon buns

Prep and cook time: 2 hours 20 minutes
Can be frozen
Makes: 24 buns

Ingredients:
800 g | 7 cups plain|all purpose flour
11 g | 2 ½ tsp easy bake yeast
200 ml | ⅞ cup milk, lukewarm
250 g | 1 ¼ cups sugar
½ tsp lemon zest
250 g | 1 ¼ cups butter, melted
2 eggs
150 g |1 cup ground almonds
2 tsp cinnamon
flour, for the work surface
100 g | ¾ cup icing|confectioners' sugar
2 tbsp lemon juice

Method:
Put the flour in a bowl and sprinkle with yeast and a pinch of salt. Add the lukewarm milk, 180 g / ¾ cup sugar, the lemon zest, half the butter and the eggs and knead to a firm dough. Continue to knead thoroughly until the dough is smooth and elastic. Cover and let rise in a warm place for 45 minutes until it has doubled in size.

Heat the oven to 200°C (180°C fan) 400°F, gas 6.

Knead the dough again, then form it to a long roll. Place the roll on a floured surface and roll it out to 1-2 cm / ½" thickness. Brush with melted butter and sprinkle with almonds. Mix the remaining sugar with the cinnamon and sprinkle evenly over the dough.

Roll the dough up lengthways. Slice into pieces 5 cm / 2" long. Place the pieces, not too close together, on a cookie sheet lined with baking parchment. Brush with the remaining butter and bake for 40 minutes until golden brown. Take out and let cool slightly.

Mix the icing/confectioners' sugar with the lemon juice and a little water to a fairly thick pouring consistency. Pour over the buns in stripes. Let dry.

Sweet brioche with sugared almonds

Prep and cook time: 1 hour 20 minutes Rising: 1 hour 20 minutes
Can be frozen
Serves: 8-10

Ingredients:
50 g | ¼ cup butter
250 g | 2 cups plain|all purpose flour
3 ½ g | ½ tsp easy bake yeast
2 eggs
1 tsp sugar
2 tbsp milk, lukewarm
75 g sugared almonds
1 egg yolk
2 tbsp cream

To decorate:
icing|confectioners' sugar

Method:

Melt the butter and let cool slightly. Place flour in a bowl and sprinkle yeast over it. Add the eggs, a pinch of salt, sugar, melted butter and lukewarm milk. Knead to a dough with the kneading hook of the electric mixer. Cover and leave in a warm place for 1 hour until the dough has doubled in size.

Heat the oven to 200°C (180°C fan) 400°F, gas 6.

Turn out the dough onto a floured work surface and knead thoroughly. Divide the dough into three and form the pieces into long rolls. Plait the rolls, press the ends together and tuck them under the brioche. Place the brioche on a cookie sheet lined with baking parchment.

Beat the egg yolk with the cream and brush it over the plait. Place the sugared almonds in the dips on the plait and press them on lightly. Let rise for a further 15-20 minutes.

Bake for 35-40 minutes. Take out of the oven and place carefully on a rack to cool.

Decorate with icing/confectioners' sugar before serving.

Sweet walnut and raisin bread

Prep and cook time: 2 hours 30 minutes
Can be frozen
Makes: 1 loaf

Ingredients:
250 g | 2 cups plain|all purpose flour
3 ½ g | ¾ tsp easy bake yeast
100 ml | 7 tbsp milk
1 tsp honey
1 egg
3 tbsp butter, melted
100 g | 1 ¼ cups chopped walnuts
50 g | ⅓ cup raisins
flour, for the work surface
milk, to brush top

Method:

Put the flour in a bowl and sprinkle over the yeast and 1 pinch of salt. Add the milk, honey, egg and butter and knead with the electric mixer or by hand to an elastic dough. If necessary, add a little lukewarm water if the dough is too dry. Cover and let rise in a warm place for 45 minutes until the dough has doubled in size.

Heat the oven to 200°C (180°C fan) 400°F, gas 6.

Knock down the dough and knead briefly, kneading in the walnut kernels and raisins. Place the dough in a buttered loaf pan and smooth the top. Cover and let rise again for at least 30 minutes.

Brush the loaf with milk and bake in the centre of the oven for 40-50 minutes until golden brown.

entertaining.

Chilli pastry hearts

Prep and cook time: 1 hour 10 minutes
Cannot be frozen
Makes: 25 - 30 hearts

Ingredients:
For the dough:
120 g | 1 cup plain|all purpose flour
$^1/_2$ tsp salt
1 pinch Cayenne pepper
75 g | $^3/_8$ cup butter
75 g | $^3/_4$ cup Parmesan cheese, grated
4 - 5 tbsp cream
flour, for the work surface

For the tomato salsa:
8 tomatoes, peeled, seeds removed
and chopped
2 shallots, chopped
1 clove garlic, chopped
2 tbsp olive oil
1 tbsp balsamic vinegar

Method:
Knead the flour, salt, Cayenne pepper, butter, Parmesan cheese and cream to a smooth dough. Wrap in cling film and chill in the fridge for 30 minutes.

Heat the oven to 200°C (180°C fan) 400°F, gas 6.

For the salsa, mix the tomatoes, shallots and garlic with the olive oil and balsamic vinegar. Season with salt and pepper. Chill.

Line a cookie sheet with baking parchment. Roll out the pastry 3-4 mm / $^1/_8$" thick, cut out hearts and lay on the cookie sheet. Bake for 10 minutes until golden brown. Cool on a wire rack and serve with the salsa.

Croustades with baked tomatoes

Prep and cook time: 1 hour 15 minutes
Cannot be frozen
Makes: 12 croustades

Ingredients:
For the croustades:
150 g | 1 ¼ cups plain|all purpose flour
½ tsp salt
1 tsp olive oil
flour, for the work surface
oil, for frying

For the baked tomatoes:
3 tomatoes, quartered
1 pinch sugar
Salt and pepper
1 - 2 tbsp garlic oil

To garnish:
12 sprigs fresh thyme

Method:
Heat the oven to 220°C (200°C fan) 425°F, gas 7.

Mix the flour and salt. Add the oil and 3-4 tbsp water and knead to a firm dough which does not stick to the bowl (add a little more flour if necessary). Wrap in cling film and let rest for 15 minutes.

Place the tomato quarters on a cookie sheet greased with olive oil. Sprinkle with salt, sugar and pepper, drizzle with olive oil and cook for 30-40 minutes on the middle shelf. Leave the oven door slightly open (using a wooden spoon handle).

Unwrap the dough and knead thoroughly for 5 minutes. Divide into 12 portions and form each into a ball. Heat the oil to 160°C.

Roll each dough ball in flour and press into a floured croustade form, hollowing out the centre so the dough sides are very thin. A mini muffin pan or a liqueur glass could also be used to form the pastry shells.

Deep-fry each croustade immediately until golden brown. Take out with a slotted spoon and drain on kitchen paper.

Take the tomatoes out of the oven. Place one tomato piece in each croustade and serve, garnished with fresh thyme.

Savoury croquettes with a yoghurt dip

Prep and cook time: 45 minutes
Cannot be frozen
Serves: 4

Ingredients:
For the croquettes:
2 tbsp butter
1 large onion, finely chopped
250 g | 2 ½ cups oatmeal
500 ml | 2 cups vegetable stock
1 tsp thyme leaves
2 tbsp fresh parsley, chopped
2 egg yolks
Tabasco
200 g | 1 lb celeriac|celery root, grated
2 tbsp walnuts, finely chopped
50 g | ½ cup wholemeal breadcrumbs
5 tbsp oil, for frying

For the yoghurt dip:
150 g | 1 ½ cups sour cream
200 g | 2 cups yoghurt
3 tbsp parsley, chopped
1 tomato, quartered, deseeded
and chopped
thyme

Method:
Heat the butter and sweat the onion until translucent. Stir in the oatmeal, stock and thyme leaves and stir until it thickens. Remove from the heat and leave to cool slightly, then stir in the parsley and egg yolks. Season with salt, pepper and a few dashes of Tabasco; leave to cool.

Stir the celeriac/celery root into the mixture with the chopped nuts. Shape the mixture into approximately 16 croquettes and coat in breadcrumbs.

Heat the oil and fry the croquettes for 12 – 15 minutes.

For the dip, mix the sour cream with the yoghurt and parsley. Stir in the tomato and season with salt and pepper.

Drain the croquettes on kitchen roll and serve with the yoghurt dip. Garnish with thyme.

Yorkshire pudding with roast beef

Prep and cook time: 1 hour 10 minutes
Cannot be frozen
Makes: 12 puddings

Ingredients:
For the roast beef:
1 tbsp clarified butter
**500 g | 1 lb roasting beef,
well trimmed**

For the Yorkshire puddings:
2 eggs
150 g | 1 ¼ cups plain|all purpose flour
300 ml | 1 ⅓ cups milk
4 tbsp lard

For the sauce:
200 g cream
2 tbsp horseradish sauce
2 tbsp lemon juice

To garnish:
black pepper
lamb's lettuce

Method:
Heat the oven to 140°C (120°C fan) 300°F, gas 2.

Heat the clarified butter in a very hot oven-proof pan and brown the beef on all sides. Roast in the oven for 30-40 minutes. Take out and season with salt and ground black pepper. Wrap in foil and let rest for 10 minutes.

For the Yorkshire puddings, beat the eggs, a pinch of salt, flour and milk with electric mixer to a smooth batter. Let rest briefly.

Turn up the oven to 250°C (230°C fan) 475°F, gas 9.

Grease a muffin tin with lard and place in the oven until the fat is bubbling. Stir the batter quickly and pour into the moulds. Bake for 12 minutes until the batter has risen and is crisp. Do not open the oven during the cooking time. Take out and let cool slightly.

For the sauce, mix the cream with the horseradish sauce and lemon juice. Season with salt and white pepper.

Slice the roast beef and arrange on the Yorkshire puddings. Place a spoonful of horseradish-cream sauce on each pudding. Sprinkle with coarse pepper and garnish with lamb's lettuce to serve.

Aubergine, tomato and mozzarella tarts

Prep and cook time: 40 minutes
Cannot be frozen
Makes: 12 tarts

Ingredients:
400 g | 14 oz puff pastry,
defrosted if frozen
200 g 1 cup sundried tomatoes, in oil
3 balls mozzarella, thinly sliced
1 aubergine|eggplant
4 tbsp pine nuts, toasted
olive oil

To garnish:
24 rocket|arugula leaves,
stalks removed

Method:

Pre-heat the oven to 200°C (180°C fan) 400°F, gas 6.

Finely chop the tomatoes, adding a little of the tomato oil, until it resembles a paste.

Roll out the puff pastry and cut out 12 circles 8 cm / 3" diameter, using a cookie cutter. Spoon some of the tomato paste on the top and season with pepper. Place a slice of mozzarella on top of the tomato paste, followed by some slices of aubergine/eggplant.

Sprinkle with a few pine nuts, drizzle olive oil over the top and place on a cookie sheet lined with baking parchment. Bake for 15-20 minutes.

When the tarts are ready, remove from the oven, garnish with a few rocket/arugula leaves and serve.

Mince pierogies

Prep and cook time: 2 hours
Cannot be frozen
Serves: 4

Ingredients:
250 g | 2 cups plain|all purpose flour
3 1/2 g | 1 tsp easy bake yeast
100 ml | 7 tbsp lukewarm milk
2 eggs
1 pinch sugar
2 tbsp oil
1 tbsp butter
1 onion, chopped
1 clove garlic, chopped
200 g | ½ lb minced beef
50 g | ½ cup mushrooms, peeled and chopped
1 egg yolk, beaten
flour, for the work surface

Method:

Sieve the flour into a bowl and sprinkle the yeast over it. Add the milk, eggs, sugar and 1 tbsp oil and knead to a dough. Cover and allow it to rise for 30 minutes.

Heat the butter with the remaining oil. Fry the onion and garlic gently. Add the mince and fry until brown and crumbly. Mix in the mushrooms and season with salt and pepper.

Heat the oven to 240°C (220°C fan) 425°F, gas 7.

Roll out the dough on a floured surface and cut out circles of 6 cm / 2 ½" diameter. Spoon a small mound of filling onto each circle, fold to make a semi-circle and press the edges down well. Place on a cookie sheet lined with baking parchment and brush with the egg yolk. Let rise for a further 15 minutes.

Bake for 15 minutes until golden brown.

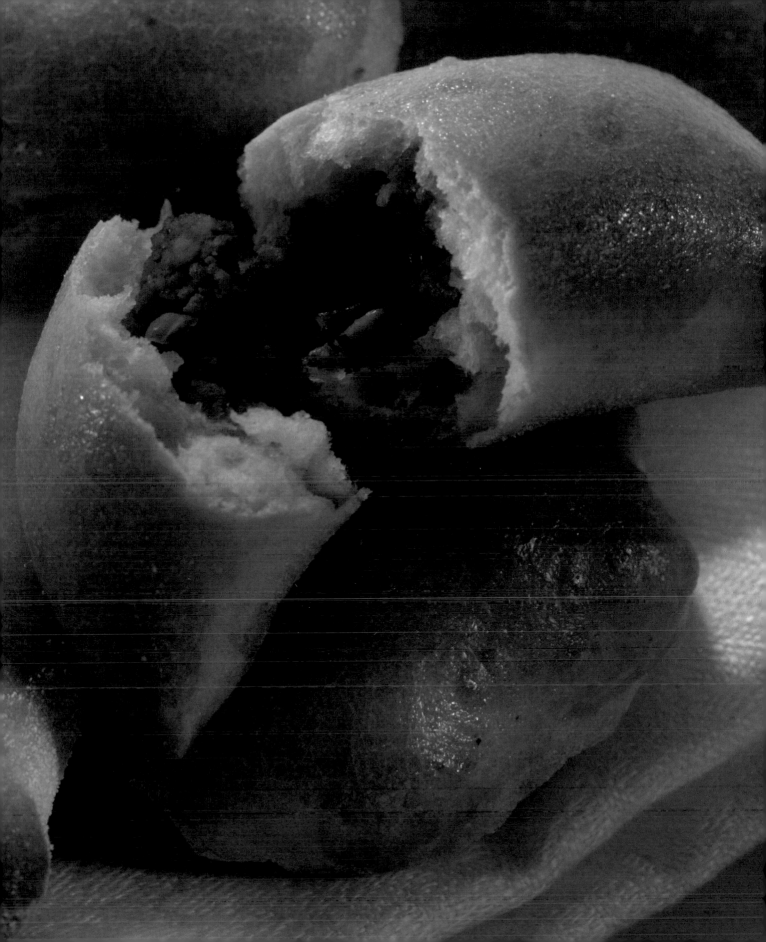

Spicy goat's cheese and chilli tarts

Prep and cook time: 30 minutes
Cannot be frozen
Makes: 12 tarts

Ingredients:
2 tbsp butter, melted
250 g | ½ lb filo pastry
1 egg white
2 red chilli peppers, seeds
removed, sliced
200 g | ¾ cup goat's cheese, chopped
1 tbsp fresh thyme leaves

Method:
Heat the oven to 220°C (200°C fan) 425°F, gas 7.

Brush the cups of a muffin pan with the melted butter.

Cut the filo pastry sheets into 24 squares of 12 cm x 12 cm / 4 ½" x 4 ½". Brush half the squares with egg white and set the rest on top, slightly offset. Press the squares carefully into the muffin pan and brush with the remaining butter.

Fill the tarts with the chilli peppers and goat's cheese. Sprinkle with a little thyme and bake for 10 minutes until golden brown.

Gougeres au fromage (choux pastries with cheese)

Prep and cook time: 1 hour
Can be frozen
Makes: 30 pastries

Ingredients:
1 pinch nutmeg
125 g | ½ cup butter
250 g | 2 cups plain|all purpose flour
4 eggs
50 g | ½ cup Gruyère, grated
egg white, for brushing
over the pastries

Method:

Heat the oven to 220°C (200°C fan) 425°F, gas 7.

Bring 250 ml / 9 fl oz / 1 ⅛ cups water to a boil with nutmeg and a pinch each of salt and pepper. Add the butter and melt. Add all the flour at once and stir well. Continue to heat the saucepan and stir thoroughly, until the dough starts to pull away from the bottom of the saucepan.

Take the saucepan off the heat and let cool slightly. Gradually beat in the eggs until a smooth dough forms. Finally, stir in about ⅔ of the cheese.

Spoon the dough into a piping bag with a large nozzle and squeeze walnut-sized mounds onto a cookie sheet lined with baking parchment. Brush with egg white and sprinkle with the rest of the cheese.

Bake for 20-25 minutes until golden brown. Let cool completely before serving.

Potato croissants with sesame and sheep's cheese filling

Prep and cook time: 1 hour
Cannot be frozen
Makes: 20 mini croissants

Ingredients:
3 medium-sized potatoes
125 g | ⅔ cup butter, melted
500 g | 4 cups plain|all purpose flour
10 g | 2 tsp baking powder
125 g | 1 cup sheep's cheese (feta)
2 tbsp chopped parsley
1 egg yolk, beaten
sesame seeds

Method:
Cook the potatoes in boiling salted water for 25 minutes.

Heat the oven to 200°C (180°C fan) 400°F, gas 6.

Drain the potatoes and press through a potato ricer while still hot. Add the butter, flour, baking powder, salt and pepper to the potatoes and knead to a dough.

Divide the dough into two halves and on a floured working surface and roll out each half to ½ cm / ¼" thick. Cut each piece into 10 triangles.

Crumble the sheep's cheese and mix with the parsley. Put one teaspoon sheep's cheese on the wide side of each triangle and roll up. Brush with beaten egg yolk and sprinkle with sesame seeds.

Bake for 20 minutes until golden brown.

Savoury tarts with tomato and apple chutney filling

Prep and cook time: 1 hour 15 minutes
Cannot be frozen
Makes: 12 tarts

Ingredients:
For the pastry:
200 g | 2 cups plain|all purpose flour
140 g | ⅝ cup butter
1 egg
1 tsp thyme leaves

For the chutney:
1 shallot, chopped
1 clove garlic, chopped
2 tbsp oil
2 apples, cored, chopped
3 tomatoes, skinned, seeds removed, chopped
5 tbsp brown sugar
1 pinch ground allspice
3 tbsp red wine vinegar
1 tsp thyme leaves
flour, for the worksurface

For the garnish:
12 sprigs thyme

Method:
For the pastry, knead all ingredients together quickly. Wrap dough in cling film and chill for 30 minutes.

For the chutney, fry the onion and garlic in oil until soft. Add the apples, tomatoes and sugar, then the allspice and vinegar. Simmer over a low heat for 20 minutes; stir occasionally and add a little water if necessary. Puree the chutney. Add the thyme, season with salt and pepper and let cool.

Heat the oven to 180°C (160°C fan) 375°F, gas 5.

Roll out the pastry on a floured surface and cut out tartlet-sized circles with a cookie cutter. Place the circles in the floured and buttered tartlet pans. Press down lightly, prick the base several times with a fork and bake for 20 minutes until golden brown.

Take the pans out of the oven and let cool for a few minutes. Take the tarts carefully out of the pans and let cool.

Fill the tarts with chutney and garnish with thyme to serve.

Almond and cherry friands

Prep and cook time: 1 hour
Cannot be frozen
Makes: 10 friands

Ingredients:
180 g | ⅞ cup butter
200 g | 1 cup sugar
60 g / ½ cup plain|all purpose flour
120 g | 1 cup ground almonds
5 egg whites
70 g | ½ cups glace cherries, chopped
1 tsp lemon zest
50 g | ⅓ cup chopped almonds

Method:
Heat the oven to 220°C (200°C fan) 425°F, gas 7.

Melt the butter and let cool slightly. Butter 10 small rectangular baking pans.

Mix sugar, flour and ground almonds in a bowl. Beat the egg whites slightly and mix with the dry ingredients.
Add the cherries, butter and lemon zest and mix well.

Fill each pan ¾ full with the dough and sprinkle with chopped almonds. Bake for 25 minutes until golden brown.

Take out and let cool for 5 minutes in the pans.
Turn out onto a wire rack to cool.

Coconut clouds with strawberry sauce

Prep and cook time: 25 minutes Freezing: 1 hour 15 minutes
Can be frozen
Serves: 4 (8 balls)

Ingredients:
400 g | 2 ¼ cups fresh
strawberries, quartered
1 tbsp strawberry liqueur
2 tbsp icing|confectioners' sugar
200 ml | ⅞ cup cream
100 g | 1 ½ cups shredded coconut
2 egg whites
70 g | ⅝ cup sugar

To decorate:
icing|confectioners' sugar

Method:
Line hemispherical moulds with plastic wrap.

Place the strawberries in a saucepan with the liqueur and the icing/confectioners' sugar. Heat for 1-2 minutes. Let cool.

Whip the cream until stiff. Fold in the coconut. Beat the egg whites with the sugar until stiff. Fold carefully into the cream. Fill loosely into a freezer bag, cut off one corner and squeeze the mixture gently and evenly into the hemispherical moulds. Freeze for at least 1 hour.

Fill half the hemispheres with the strawberry sauce. Take the other half out of the moulds and put together with the filled halves. Press the halves together lightly. Freeze for at least 15 minutes.

Remove the balls from the moulds and place on plates. Pull off the plastic wrap and dust lightly with icing/confectioners' sugar. Break open one ball and serve at once.

Macaroons

Prep and cook time: 55 minutes
Cannot be frozen
Makes: 40 - 50 macaroons

Ingredients:
3 egg whites
125 g | 1 ⅛ cups icing|confectioners' sugar
200 g | ½ lb marzipan paste
75 g | ¾ cup shredded coconut
20 ml | 4 tsp rum

To decorate:
100 g | ¼ lb dark chocolate, chopped

Method:
Heat the oven to 180°C (160°C) 375°F, gas 5.

Beat the egg whites with a pinch of salt until stiff. Stir in half the icing/confectioners' sugar and the marzipan paste. Then add the remaining icing/confectioners' sugar, shredded coconut and rum and mix to form a stiff dough.

Using two spoons, place heaps of dough on a cookie sheet lined with baking paper. Bake for 20-25 minutes until golden brown.

Take the macaroons out of the oven and let cool. Melt the chocolate in a bowl set over a pan of hot water. Decorate the macaroons with stripes of melted chocolate. Place macaroons on baking parchment and let cool completely.

Gingerbread with sugar pearls

Prep and cook time: 1 hour 15 minutes
Cannot be frozen
Makes: 35 - 40 biscuits

Ingredients:
250 g | 2 cups plain|all purpose flour
1 tsp baking powder
175 g | ⁷/₈ cup brown sugar
1 egg
1 tbsp liquid honey
1 tsp cinnamon
¹/₂ tsp ground ginger
1 tbsp candied lemon peel, chopped
50 g ¹/₂ cup ground almonds
3 tbsp milk
60 g | ¹/₄ cup butter

For the icing:
200 g | 1 ³/₄ cups icing|confectioners' sugar

To decorate:
sugar pearls

Method:

Mix the flour, baking powder, sugar and salt with the egg, honey, cinnamon and ginger in a mixing bowl. Add the candied peel, ground almonds and milk. Dot the mixture with small pieces of butter and knead to a dough with the kneading hook of the electric mixer.

Turn the dough out onto a floured surface and continue to knead by hand until smooth. Shape into two rolls of 3 cm / 1" diameter each. Wrap the rolls in foil and leave in a cool place for 1 hour.

Heat the oven to 200°C (180°C fan) 400°F, gas 6.

Chop the rolls into slices 2 cm / ¹/₂" thick. Lay the slices, not too close together, on a cookie sheet lined with baking parchment. Bake for 15 minutes. Take out and cool on a wire rack.

For the icing, mix the icing/confectioners' sugar with 4 tbsp water to a thick pouring consistency. Brush the gingerbread with the icing. Sprinkle with sugar pearls and let the icing set.

Brownies with walnuts

Prep and cook time: 50 minutes
Can be frozen
Makes: 30 brownies

Ingredients:
250 g | 1 cups dark
chocolate, chopped
180 g | ¾ cup butter
150 g | 1 ¼ cup icing|confectioners'
sugar
200 g | 1 ⅔ cups plain|all purpose flour
2 tbsp cocoa
100 g | ¾ cups walnuts,
roughly chopped
1 tsp baking powder
1 pinch of salt
3 eggs
80 g | 2 tbsp maple syrup
2 tsp vanilla extract

Method:
Heat the oven to 160°C (140°C fan) 325°F, gas 3.

Melt ⅔ cup of the chocolate with the butter in a small pan.

Put the icing/confectioners' sugar, flour, cocoa, nuts, baking powder and salt into a bowl. Beat in the eggs, maple syrup, vanilla extract and melted chocolate-butter mix. Stir the rest of the chocolate into the mixture.

Turn the mixture into a baking pan lined with baking parchment and bake for 20-30 minutes. Take out, leave to cool slightly then take out of the tin and leave to cool completely.

Cut into squares to serve.

Baklava

Prep and cook time: 50 minutes
Cannot be frozen
Serves: 4

Ingredients:
250 g | ½ lb filo pastry
100 g | ¾ cup walnuts
50 g | ⅓ cup almonds
50 g | ⅓ cup pistachios
1 egg white
2 tbsp honey
½ tsp cinnamon
1 tsp rose water
50 g | ¼ cup butter, melted
125 g | ⅗ cup sugar
2 tbsp lemon juice

Method:

Heat the oven to 220°C (200°C fan) 425°F, gas 7.

Carefully separate the pastry sheets. Cut each sheet to the pan size and cover with a damp cloth.

Chop the walnuts and almonds finely in the blender. Chop the pistachios less finely.

Beat the egg white until stiff. Fold in the honey, nuts, cinnamon and rose water. Butter the pan and line with alternate layers of pastry sheets and nut mixture, brushing each pastry sheet with melted butter. Finish with 2-3 pastry sheets.

Bake for 30 minutes. Meanwhile, bring the sugar to a boil with 125 ml / ⅝ cup water. Simmer for 1 minute. Remove from heat, let cool slightly and stir in the lemon juice.

Take the baklava out of the oven. While it is still hot, pour the syrup over gradually. Let cool.

To serve, take out of the pan and cut into diamond shapes.

Chocolate dipped coconut macaroons

Prep and cook time: 1 hour
Cannot be frozen
Makes: 30 - 35 macaroons

Ingredients:
3 egg whites
80 g | 1/3 cup sugar
2 tsp lemon juice
175 g | 1 1/2 cups shredded coconut
100 g | 2/3 cups dark
chocolate, chopped

Method:

Heat the oven to 150°C (130°C fan) 300°F, gas 2.

Beat the egg whites until stiff. Add the sugar gradually and continue to beat until stiff. Stir in the lemon juice. Fold in the shredded coconut.

Using two teaspoons, place small mounds of the mixture not too close together onto a cookie sheet lined with baking parchment. Wet a plastic bowl scraper and your finger tips with water and shape each mound to a pyramid.

Bake the macaroons for 20 minutes. They should only brown lightly, so cover with baking parchment or foil if necessary. Take out and let cool.

Melt the chocolate in a bowl over a saucepan of hot water. Dip the bottom of the macaroons in the melted chocolate and let dry on baking parchment.

Butter cookies with raspberries

Prep and cook time: 1 hour
Cannot be frozen
Makes: 40 - 50 cookies

Ingredients:
Cookie dough:
400 g | 3 ½ cups plain|all purpose flour
125 g | ⅔ cup sugar
1 - 2 tsp vanilla extract
250 g | 1 cup butter
4 egg yolks

In addition:
Flour, for working
250 g | 1 cup raspberry jam (jelly)
200 g | 1 ½ cups raspberries

Method:

Combine all the dough ingredients and quickly knead to a smooth dough. Add a little ice-cold water if the dough is too crumbly. Wrap in cling film and chill for at least 1 hour.

Heat the oven to 180°C (160°C fan) 375°F, gas 5.

Divide the dough into two portions and roll each portion into a sausage, 4 cm / 1 ½" in diameter. Cut into slices about 1 cm / ½" thick and flatten slightly. Put onto a cookie sheet lined with baking parchment and bake for 15-20 minutes, until nicely browned.

Take off the sheet and leave to cool completely. Push the raspberry jam through a sieve and put a blob on top of each cookie. Add two raspberries to each and press on lightly.

index

index.

index.